SO, YOU WANT To Work in FASHION?

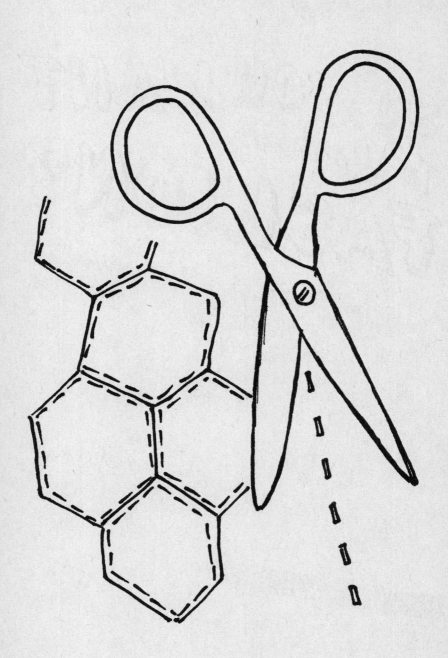

SO, YOU WANT To Work in FASHION?

How to Break into the World of FASHION AND DESIGN

patricia Wooster

BE WHAT YOU WANT series

ALADDIN
New York London Toronto Sydney New Delhi

BEYOND WORDS
Hillsboro, Oregon

ALADDIN
An imprint of Simon & Schuster
Children's Publishing Division
1230 Avenue of the Americas
New York, NY 10020

BEYOND WORDS
20827 N.W. Cornell Road, Suite 500
Hillsboro, Oregon 97124-9808
503-531-8700 / 503-531-8773 fax
www.beyondword.com

This Beyond Words/Aladdin edition September 2014
Text copyright © 2014 by Beyond Words/Simon & Schuster, Inc.
Illustrations copyright © 2014 by iStockphoto.com
Cover photo copyright © 2014 by Plainpicture/Glow Images

For information about special discounts for bulk purchases, please contact Simon &
Schuster Special Sales at 1-866-506-1949 or business@simonandschuster.com.

The Simon & Schuster Speakers Bureau can bring authors to your live event.
For more information or to book an event contact the Simon & Schuster Speakers
Bureau at 1-866-248-3049 or visit our website at www.simonspeakers.com.

Managing Editor: Lindsay S. Brown
Copyeditor: Kristin Thiel
Proofreader: Gretchen Stelter
Design: Sara E. Blum
The text of this book was set in Bembo and Interstate.

Manufactured in the United States of America 0814 FFG

10 9 8 7 6 5 4 3 2 1

Library of Congress Cataloging-in-Publication Data

Wooster, Patricia.
  So, you want to work in fashion? : how to break into the world of fashion
    and design / Patricia Wooster.
  pages   cm. — (Be what you want series)
  Includes bibliographical references.
  1. Fashion—Vocational guidance—Juvenile literature. I. Title.
TT507.W6674 2014
746.9'2023—dc23

2014005268

ISBN 978-1-58270-453-1 (hc)
ISBN 978-1-58270-452-4 (pbk)
ISBN 978-1-4814-0113-5 (eBook)

CONTENTS

1

A Closetful of Options

Imagine having passes to see all of the runway shows at New York Fashion Week. Or picture yourself opening up *Vogue* magazine and seeing a model wearing fantastic clothes and knowing you were a part of making that photo happen. In these scenarios, where do you see yourself? Are you a famous fashion designer? A supermodel? Did you photograph the clothes? Maybe your job is to write about the clothes for buyers.

The fashion industry is a fast-paced and exciting place to be. If you love clothes and have a strong sense of style, then you might want to consider a career in fashion. There are a lot of different career fields in fashion—but it's a very competitive environment. With a lot of hard work and some planning, you can enjoy all that this industry has to offer. See if any of the five fashion fields below inspires you and makes you want to dive into the wonderful world of fashion.

Reasons You May Want to Work in Fashion

You Love to Be Creative

Do you love to make beautiful things? Are you constantly sketching ideas for new clothes? Do you see the clothes people are wearing and think of ways you could alter them into something new? A person who wants to create new clothes must have a strong imagination. A designer decides the style, cut, and fit of the clothes, and knows about fabrics and industry trends. There's a lot to learn, but seeing your designs come down the runway is a huge reward!

You Love to Make Stuff

Do you like to keep a low profile and work behind the scenes? Do you like to work with patterns, cut fabric, or sew? Would you rather someone else come up with the designs, so you can put them together? Are you good at working as a team? Putting a garment together involves a lot of people. There's a huge demand for patternmakers, fabric cutters, and garment makers.

You Love to Make Decisions

Are you interested in fashion and business? Do you enjoy gathering information and reading research reports? Can you juggle multiple projects? Are you good at making decisions? If you have a head for numbers and an appreciation for fashion, then a career in merchandising may be for you. This broad field includes retail management, store buyer, advertising executive, and promoter.

You Love to Talk about Fashion

Do you love to write or take pictures? Are you interested in fashion news, trends, and designers? Can you spend hours sitting at a computer? Are you good at coming up with ideas? Lots of people depend on fashion writers and photographers. A person in this field can work in advertising, write a blog, or work at a fashion magazine.

You Love to Dress Up

Do people often comment on how you dress? Are you good at combining clothing with accessories to make a great outfit? Can you put clothing from different stores and different price ranges together and make a cohesive outfit that works? As a stylist, you might be asked to put fashion looks together for an individual shopper, a photo shoot, or a showroom window. If you are confident and love to shop, this may be a great career for you.

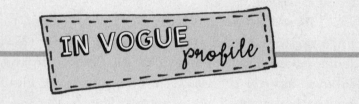

Name: Jeffrey Sebelia
Job: Fashion designer

AFTER HIS BAND, LIFTER, BROKE UP, JEFFREY SEBELIA ENROLLED IN SEWING CLASSES AT THE LOS ANGELES TRADE TECHNICAL COLLEGE. HIS MUSICAL BACKGROUND INFLUENCED HIS CLOTHING LINE COSA NOSTRA, WHICH WAS WORN BY SINGERS LIKE DAVE NAVARRO, TOMMY LEE, AND JENNIFER LOPEZ. IN 2006 HE AUDITIONED FOR THE DESIGN SHOW *PROJECT RUNWAY* AND WAS CHOSEN AS A CONTESTANT. THE RESIDENT "BAD BOY" WON SEASON THREE OF THE SHOW AND WAS FEATURED IN *ELLE* MAGAZINE. IN 2009 *CLICHÉ* MAGAZINE NAMED HIM ONE OF THE MOST PROMINENT DESIGNERS OF HIS GENERATION. HIS NEW CLOTHING LINE FOR KIDS, LA MINIATURA, COMBINES LATE-1970S POST–PUNK ROCK WITH PREPPY DETAILS. HIS LOVE OF MUSIC CONTINUES TO BE AN INSPIRATION.

3

What was the biggest challenge of being on *Project Runway*?

The [design] challenges were very hard for me. I have never been the best at sewing fast, and I've never considered myself to be a dressmaker. I strive each day in my company to improve and hone my design ability, and I know everything there is to know about garment construction, but in the real world, I spend my days working on design, costing, production, textiles, and merchandising, not sewing.

How did your career change after you won?

Because *Project Runway* is so popular, just being on the show helped get me interviews and opportunities I know I wouldn't have had otherwise. That being said, there is also a stigma attached that most people couldn't imagine. The fashion industry seems to have a love/hate relationship with *Project Runway*. While most who work in fashion will admit to loving the show, they are also a bit skeptical about what it means and don't quite trust its authenticity. I personally have mixed feelings about it . . . because no matter how many challenges I've won, I know that my design ability reaches far beyond my sewing ability and that the time constraints inherent in *Project Runway* mean it is really a game show before anything else.

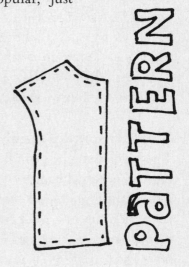

What have you been up to since *Project Runway* ended?

In the seven and a half years since season three, I have built and sold a contemporary fashion label business and am currently building a children's lifestyle brand.

Where do you get your inspiration for designing clothing?
Inspiration for me comes from all over the place. But for the last year and a half, my fiancée has been my muse.

How is designing clothing for kids different from designing for adults?
At its base, there is nothing different. As a designer, I constantly try to put myself in the customer's shoes and do research to learn as much as I can while removing my needs, so that I am not designing for me but for the customer. With kids, I just have a whole new type of customer who has so many different needs from me that have to be addressed. When I picture the La Miniatura kid throughout his or her day, I consider the week . . . school, after-school activities like sports and clubs, summer camp, holidays, birthdays, etc. I also draw on my childhood and my experience with my son.

What are some of the biggest challenges in this business?
The biggest challenge in the kid's business as I see it is navigating the personal baggage of buyers and parents. For instance, I constantly am asked to use less red or purple in my boy's collection because most buyers and parents see these as feminine colors. Meanwhile, I poll my son and his friends (both boys and girls), and I have found that kids love color and don't attach any gender identification with colors.

What has been one of the most exciting moments you've had since starting in this industry?
Each business I have started or been involved with seems to be exciting in the beginning. When starting Cosa Nostra years ago, it was exciting to have people like Elton John, Winona Ryder, John Galliano, and Karl Lagerfeld buy my clothes. Now it's exciting taking La Miniatura and opening doors like Harrods, Selfridges, Harvey Nichols, and Bergdorf Goodman.

Who would you like to see wearing your clothes?
As many kids as possible.

What advice would you give aspiring designers?
Be obsessed! Be humble and learn as much as you can, and as long as you have the drive . . . don't give up. The reward is well worth the hard work.

I enjoy the speed of fashion. I love doing different things, and I think I still have something valid to say in fashion.

Tom Ford★

FASHION IS BIG BUSINESS[1]

- The fashion industry employs 4.2 million people.
- Only 19,300 of the people who work in fashion are fashion designers.
- The average fashion designer makes $62,610 a year.
- Americans spend $250 billion on fashion every year.
- Globally, fashion is a $1.2 trillion industry.
- Clothing accessories make up $16.5 billion of the market.
- Americans spend $34.1 billion a year on clothing and accessories at online retail stores.

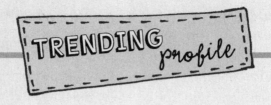

Name: Courtney Allegra
Age: 16
Job (when not studying!): Fashion designer

DOES THE THOUGHT OF CREATING SIXTY DIFFERENT CLOTHING LOOKS IN ONE YEAR SEEM EXCITING? WHAT IF YOU'RE ALSO AN EQUESTRIAN AND A HIGH SCHOOL STUDENT? TO MOST PEOPLE, THIS MAY SEEM LIKE A LOT, BUT COURTNEY ALLEGRA IS ACCOMPLISHING IT. HER VIBRANT AND WELL-TAILORED CLOTHES HAVE APPEARED AT LOS ANGELES FASHION WEEK AND IN SEVENTEEN MAGAZINE. IN 2013 SHE WAS INVITED TO APPEAR ON THE TODAY SHOW AS A PART OF THE "STARS FOR TOMORROW" SEGMENT. SHE DRESSES CELEBRITIES AND FRIENDS OF ALL AGES AND SIZES. WHAT STARTED AS A HOBBY ALLEGRA SHARED WITH FAMILY AND FRIENDS HAS TURNED INTO A BUDDING CAREER.

When did you discover your love for fashion and designing?
I've always been into fashion and drawing sketches, but it wasn't until I was fifteen that I got serious about designing. A family friend who knows I love fashion asked me to debut a clothing line at a show in Los Angeles during fashion week. Obviously I said yes, and I had to create ten looks in only two weeks! My line was very well received. After the show, lots of people were interviewing me and just asking where to buy my clothes. And that's when I figured out that I had to make a website if my designing was going to be serious.

How do you balance school and work responsibilities?
It's challenging, to say the least. This year, my junior year, I'm taking online classes rather than physically going to high school. It's way easier as far as time goes because I can meet certain deadlines for fashion shows and whatnot without missing school. I also have more time for my horses and animals now!

Where do you find inspiration for your fashion design?
I find inspiration in everything. My favorite movies, other people's styles, magazines, shopping for fabrics, and especially traveling.

What do you like most about having your own line?
The thing I like the most about having my own line is being in charge. If I were working for another designer or fashion house, I wouldn't be able to have the freedom to create whatever I want. I love having my own line because there are no limits and I can be as creative as I want.

What is the most challenging thing about having your own line?
The most challenging is working with manufacturers. Now that my business has grown, I had to pick some manufacturers to work with. When I started designing for men, I thought that was going to be a bigger challenge, but it isn't. It's hard to communicate exact ideas to manufacturers, so I always have to go to Los Angeles to supervise and fit the clothes.

What has been one of the most exciting moments you've had since starting your fashion career?
One of the most exciting moments was showing my line on Fashion Minga's runway! It was the debut of my line CA11, which is a men's and women's urban punk line.

What advice can you give other kids who are interested in a fashion career?
If you want to be in fashion, you have to be determined, focused, and confident. Don't follow the trends if you don't want to. Honestly, there are no real trends anymore. If you walk down the street, everyone has different styles, and most people could care less about trends. Design what you want!

FASHION JOBS TEENAGERS ARE DOING RIGHT NOW

- ✂ Accessories designer
- ✂ Blogger
- ✂ Clothing designer
- ✂ Fashion editor
- ✂ Fashion illustrator
- ✂ Model
- ✂ Photographer
- ✂ Retail
- ✂ Stylist
- ✂ Vlogger

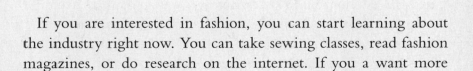

If you are interested in fashion, you can start learning about the industry right now. You can take sewing classes, read fashion magazines, or do research on the internet. If you a want more hands-on experience, start a blog, sketch clothing designs, or create a portfolio of photographs.

Name: Cecilia Cassini
Age: 14
Job (when not studying!): Fashion designer

CECILIA CASSINI IS ONE OF THE YOUNGEST DESIGNERS IN THE WORLD TO SEE HER CLOTHES WALK DOWN THE RUNWAY. IN THIRD GRADE, WHEN OTHER KIDS WERE READING CHAPTER BOOKS, SHE WAS WRITING A BOOK REPORT ON *THE DEVIL WEARS PRADA*. HER FASHION LABEL LAUNCHED IN 2009, WHEN SHE WAS NINE YEARS OLD. BY THE TIME SHE WAS ELEVEN, SHE HAD DESIGNED OVER FIVE HUNDRED PIECES FOR GIRLS AGES FOUR TO FOURTEEN. SHE IS PASSIONATE ABOUT FASHION DESIGN AND ENCOURAGES OTHER KIDS TO FOLLOW THEIR DREAMS. AS A ROLE MODEL, SHE INSPIRES KIDS BY SPEAKING AT ELEMENTARY SCHOOLS, HOSPITALS, AND SHELTERS. HER CHARITABLE WORK LANDED HER A PRUDENTIAL SPIRIT OF COMMUNITY AWARD IN 2012. CECILIA IS A PERFECT EXAMPLE OF HOW YOU'RE NEVER TOO YOUNG TO FOLLOW YOUR DREAMS!

When did you discover your love for fashion and designing?
I truly believe that I was born with fashion in my blood. Ever since I can remember, I have always been obsessed with fashion and fabulous clothing. When I was in preschool, I used to paint flowers and rainbows on my dresses instead of on the paper on the easels. By the time I was about four, I was embroidering my clothing. When I was five, I began cutting

up my clothing (or my mom's or sister's) and repurposing them into new and fabulous creations. I remember I would hem the dresses with hair clips, and I would sew the different pieces together with ponytail holders. Finally, when I was six, I got my first sewing machine, and that is when I really began to be able to design and create my fashion.

How do you balance school and work responsibilities?
In order to handle my school and fashion responsibilities, I need to be very organized and manage my time wisely. It is important to me that I do well in school, so I always make sure to stay on top of my workload and never get behind. When I can, I even work ahead so that when I am inspired, I will have time to design and create. When I know I have a specific event coming up for my fashion, I plan ahead.

What do you like most about working in fashion?
The best thing about my job is that I have never considered my designing a job! Fashion and designing are my hugest passions, and I absolutely love what I do. To me, a job is something you have to do. I am lucky because I love designing. In fact, I think I live, breathe, and love it more than anything else I could spend my time doing. The other great thing about my "job" is that I get the opportunity to meet so many talented people along the way. Everyone I have met in the business—from Betsey Johnson to Heidi Klum to Taylor Swift to Sofia Vergara to Diane von Furstenburg—have been so supportive of my dreams and my work.

Also, as part of my "job," I speak to hundreds of kids a year in my Follow Your Dreams campaign, where I encourage all young people to find their passion and to begin following their dreams now—rather than waiting until they grow up. Part of my Follow Your Dreams campaign includes giving dresses to needy girls at hospitals, shelters, or schools because every little girl deserves a dress, so that is very rewarding for me—to be able to help someone and to be able to give back. Because of my sponsorship with Singer SVP, I also donate a Singer sewing machine to each place I visit, so hopefully the kids will learn the art of sewing and be empowered by being able to design and create their own fashion. As you can see, my "job"—if you are going to call it a job—is the best one anyone can have.

What is the most challenging thing about working in fashion?
Sometimes the pressure to be able to design something for someone when I am not inspired is challenging. No matter what, I have the pressure to design something fabulous, and that can be scary when I am not feeling inspired. Also, the responsibilities and pressures that go along with my age (I am fourteen) are sometimes a challenge for me when I am designing.

What has been one of the most exciting moments you've had since starting your fashion career?
Some of the most exciting moments I have had since I started selling my designs at age ten have been going to New York Fashion Week, being featured in worldwide fashion magazines (*Vogue* France; *Elle* Japan; *Grazia* Italy, England, Germany; *New York Times*; *People* magazine; *Glamour*, etc.), and having a show on the Style Network. Most of all, seeing people wearing my Cecilia Cassini designs is really the most thrilling.

Where do you see yourself in ten years?
In ten years I will be finished with university, and I will be a pro at showing my collections at fashion weeks around the world—from Milan to Paris to New York. I will also have Cecilia Cassini stores around the world.

What advice can you give other kids who are interested in a fashion career?

My advice to other kids who want to get started in fashion is follow your dreams. You don't have to wait to be an adult to follow your dreams, so get started now! If you have the passion, the motivation, the work ethic, and the inspiration, anything is possible. Go for it!

Rafi Ridwan: Hearing Color

If you asked Rafi Ridwan if it's possible to follow your dreams at a young age, he'd say yes. Born deaf, he has learned to hear sound through color. At the age of six, he discovered his love for fashion while watching Disney's *The Little Mermaid*. He didn't like the clothes Ariel was wearing in the movie, so he began sketching a new wardrobe for her. When he was nine, he attended a fashion festival and showed his designs to famous Indonesian fashion designer Barli Asmara. Asmara recognized Ridwan's talent and created a collection with him. As Indonesia's youngest fashion designer, he was given the opportunity to appear on *America's Next Top Model* when the show was filmed in Bali in 2013. Tyra Banks named him the "newest, fiercest fashion designer in the world."[2] Ridwan is a role model in his community, and earned a lot of respect when he used his fellow hearing-impaired classmates to model his clothes at a fashion show. His dream is to show his designs at the fashion shows in Milan, Paris, and Japan. At only eleven years old, he's already very close to achieving his dreams.

Fashion is not something that exists in dresses only. Fashion is in the sky, in the street; fashion has to do with ideas, the way we live, what is happening.

COCO CHANEL[*]

2

Get Schooled in Fashion

Now that you've decided to explore the fashion industry, where do you begin? With a little research, of course! This book provides you with information about a lot of different career fields in fashion. Some focus on creativity: designer, photographer, model, and stylist. Other careers handle the business side of fashion: construction, promotion, and retail buying. Whatever your interests are, the fashion industry has a career for you.

What is the one quality all of these careers share? They all share a love for fashion. Most people think of designing clothes when they first start thinking about a career in fashion. This is the job with the most visibility. This is the job that is the most competitive. A lot of different types of people with different careers are necessary to support a designer. Someone must produce the clothes. Someone else has to model, photograph, and advertise them, not to mention the retail stores who buy and sell the clothing. All of these jobs require different skills and training. And all of these jobs have been done by kids just like you!

Smart Options for Stylish Kids

Opportunities to learn about fashion are everywhere. You just need to know where to look!

I'm useless at staring at a piece of white paper. But if you put a piece of white paper with a black line on it in front of me, I'll say, no, that black line should be red, and it should go this way or that way.

MARC JACOBS*

CAMP FASHION DESIGN

If you are a fan of the show *Project Runway* and love a good challenge, then Camp Fashion Design may be the camp for you. Located in New York City, campers get to visit the Garment District and the famous Mood Fabrics store. Daily challenges test your creativity and teach you new ways to create fashion. Representatives from some of the major fashion design schools like Parsons The New School for Design, Fashion Institute of Design & Merchandising (FIDM), and Fashion Institute of Technology (FIT) often meet and speak with campers. The camp ends with a fashion show for your friends and family where you can show off your new designs.

Cut Loose

You can find a fashion-related camp almost anywhere. Some are focused on fashion design, others on modeling and photography. Camps range from day programs to overnight experiences. Some of these camps are held at art schools and universities. New York City offers several exciting opportunities where campers visit fashion showrooms, meet fashion executives, and create their own fashion brand.

Just Another Mannequin Monday

If you're looking for a local experience, take a class at a fabric store or a place that sells sewing machines. They will teach you how to use a machine, pick fabrics, and cut patterns. After you learn the basics, you can usually find advanced classes where you may learn to sew a pair of pants or create a purse. Even if your area of interest in fashion is not sewing, it's always good to know the basics of how a garment is constructed.

Virtually Fashionable

If you are looking for a little fashion fun, play a fantasy game on your computer. (Check with your parents before doing anything online.) Fashion Fantasy Game allows you to pretend to be a fashion stylist, designer, or store owner. You can chat with other people interested in fashion while growing your skills in fashion and business. The *Teen Vogue* Me Girl app for mobile devices lets you imagine what it would be like to intern for *Teen Vogue* magazine. Your character goes on various styling assignments and photo shoots, and you are scored based on how well your models are styled. Both games let you chat online with other people playing the game. You can share your designs along with your fashion interests with kids across the globe.

BE A STAR

In 2008 fashion designer Vivienne Tam teamed up with the creators of Stardoll to launch a website for teens interested in fashion. Tam hosted online chats and picked one lucky aspiring designer to visit her design studio and watch her work. Since then, Stardoll has grown to become the world's largest fashion design game. Users can dress their own MeDoll using clothes and accessories that are currently on trend. You can take the game a step further by using the StarDesign Fashion application to create your own clothes. It's a very social community of teens, so be prepared to chat about fashion!

Fashion Forward: Getting Your Degree

Associate Degree (AA, AAS)
Many art and design schools offer a two-year degree in fashion studies. This degree is best for students hoping to start with an entry-level job in fashion or for students who aren't interested in a four-year program.

Bachelor Degree (BA, BS)
Bachelor degrees are offered at universities and most art colleges. These four-year degrees allow students to take fashion classes along with general liberal arts courses. Earning this degree will give you a great foundation in fashion, along with career versatility.

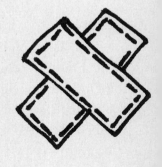

Bachelor of Fine Arts (BFA)

This four-year degree can be found at most art colleges and some universities. The emphasis in this program is on studio time over class lectures. Students spend a lot of time completing projects and practicing their craft. This degree is an excellent option for people who know exactly what kind of career they want and want to focus on hands-on experience.

Master of Fine Arts Degree (MFA)

This is a two- to three-year program where students can dig deeper into the fashion world. They take classes in trend analysis, marketing, and computer technology to enhance their work. Hands-on studio time is emphasized. Students complete a final project, which may be a fashion portfolio or fashion collection.

Master of Design in Fashion, Body, and Garments (MDes)

Fashion and research are combined in this two-year program. Students follow a structured class schedule and examine how film, art, and music influence fashion. Each year students are usually required to turn in a body of work influenced by their studies from that year. This is a wonderful program for students interested in examining various art forms and inspirations.

FIVE VS. FIVE

There are good reasons to get a general education, as can be found with a Bachelor of Arts (BA) degree, and there are good reasons to get a fashion-focused education, as can be found with a Bachelor of Fine Arts (BFA) degree.

Five Reasons to Get a BA

1. Two-thirds of classes are general studies courses in liberal arts.

2. There is more flexibility in choosing what classes to take.

3. A well-rounded education may lead to more career opportunities.

4. You receive more exposure to history, logic, and humanities courses, which may help creativity.

5. The focus is more on academics and less on studio time.

Five Reasons to Get a BFA

1. Two-thirds of classes are visual arts courses.

2. You take classes more focused in your area of interest.

3. You get a professional degree instead of one in general studies.

4. You receive more preprofessional training.

5. The focus is more on studio time than on academics.

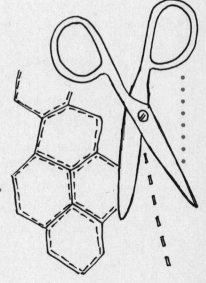

Name: Lindsay Giambattista
Age: 25
Job: Fashion philanthropist

IN 2005, LINDSAY GIAMBATTISTA HAD A DREAM TO OUTFIT GIRLS WHO DON'T HAVE MUCH MONEY IN THE LATEST FASHIONS FOR FREE. IT WAS A PRETTY BIG DREAM FOR A FOURTEEN-YEAR-OLD, BUT THAT DIDN'T STOP GIAMBATTISTA FROM OPENING TAYLOR'S CLOSET, A PLACE WHERE TEENS CAN SHOP FREE OF CHARGE. SINCE THEN TAYLOR'S CLOSET HAS HELPED OVER TWELVE THOUSAND GIRLS BY GIVING AWAY OVER $1 MILLION IN CLOTHES. IN ADDITION, TAYLOR'S CLOSET PROVIDES CLASSES, GUIDANCE, AND FRIENDSHIP. IN 2011, GIAMBATTISTA TOOK ANOTHER STEP FORWARD IN HER FASHION CAREER BY STARTING HER BACHELOR OF FINE ARTS IN FASHION FROM THE SAVANNAH COLLEGE OF ART AND DESIGN (SCAD). SHE PLANS TO PURSUE A CAREER WHERE SHE CAN CONTINUE TO COMBINE FASHION AND PHILANTHROPY.

When did you discover your love for fashion and designing?

I've always had an affinity for the creative. My dad is a graphic designer and advertising expert, so I grew up always thinking and problem solving through discussion and creative thinking. It wasn't until I was a little bit older that I realized fashion is an extension of that. My mom and I always tried on outfits together, piecing together ensembles in stores. It became something that I really loved. As I grew up, I started realizing this was something all women related to, and there was something deeper happening when I tried on clothes or picked out a new outfit.

How did the idea of Taylor's Closet fulfill that passion?
It was the most natural transition. I began noticing how happy
I was trying on these beautiful garments. I noticed how it made
me feel beautiful and feminine in a strong way. I was fourteen
at the time, so I probably couldn't have put it into those words.
However, I just noticed something different about my attitude
when I interacted with clothing. It got me thinking about
other girls my age. I started wondering if there were other
girls out there who felt the same feeling I did when they tried
on clothes. I wondered if they had a love for all things girly but
couldn't access it like I could. It just hit me one day. I needed
to start giving away these clothes of mine, so that other girls
in different circumstances could experience what I felt: feeling
beautiful and worth it. We've grown to only carry brand-new
designer clothing. As we grow, our mission continues to sur-
round the idea of going to great lengths to show girls how
important and worthy they are despite their circumstances.

How do you balance school and work responsibilities?
Handling school and work at the same time has been a huge
learning experience for me. I am notoriously a perfectionist,
and I've had to learn the science of letting things go. The reality of time is that sometimes there isn't enough of it to make
every detail perfect. So instead of perfection, I try to strive for
excellence, which is a bit less daunting and still leaves room for
error. But I do have to say, I find the challenge to be refreshing
sometimes. I like to see the capacity in which you can push
yourself when given an overwhelming amount of work—I
think it allows for a detail-orientated work ethic that makes
the end result so much better. But what goes along with that
is learning balance. As I've progressed in school,
I've realized that work is just one part of life.
Friends, family, God, and obviously taking
care of yourself are the backbone to life.
What you do as your work is the extra stuff
that adds to it.

What is the most rewarding aspect of your school program?

Construction is the most rewarding. I have an enormous amount of respect for the patternmakers and seamstresses of the industry, because I see how hands-on and intense it is to create a simple garment that then gets produced en masse and sold. It is the most meticulous, technical, time-consuming, artistic process to create a pattern from scratch, cut, and construct it into a garment. Therefore, sketching an idea and then actually making it with your own two hands is an extremely satisfying process.

What is the most challenging thing about your school program?

All of the work I do at my school is challenging. The amount of time we are given to execute projects is very short, which leaves little room for free time. Although, I would have to say one of the most challenging aspects of my school program is our garment construction curriculum. SCAD focuses heavily on teaching how to construct garments, so that, as designers, we can communicate properly with patternmakers and seamstresses. Our projects and finals consist of finished, sewn garments all executed by us. I am a designer/creative at heart, and therefore, the technical part of my curriculum is more difficult for me. However, it's so crucial for us to know and learn if we want to be successful. The most renowned designers always studied tailoring or construction before they launched in design.

What has been one of the most exciting moments you've had since starting your fashion career?

I am still so new in this big industry! I've loved just getting small glimpses of how things work and the certain types of companies that I would love to model. One of the most incredible experiences I've had was interning at Helmut Lang. I was privileged to be in the patternmaking department. I became part of such an incredible team who were some of the most skilled craftsman and also respected one another and treated each other like family. The most exciting process was seeing the designers bring a very rough sketch to the pattern-makers and watching how that idea would ultimately be made into a garment, walk down the runway, and then be sold to their loyal customer base. It was thrilling to watch. I can't tell you how much I learned seeing the amount of hands it takes to successfully run an apparel company.

What advice would you give kids who are interested in going to fashion school?

First, if you are serious about design and fashion, be willing to work very hard. Be willing to push yourself. However, know that sometimes even if you work hard and push your-self, you are still going to fail. It's good to keep in mind that if you learn from the failure, that cycle will end up teaching you a lot about your aesthetic and ultimately where you will want to end up in your career. Second, this is so cliché, but I think it needs to be said: be you. In the way you work, in the way you think, and in the way you design. I think we fashion students can be guided too heavily by trends and market research. Remember that your own ideas, constructed from your own experiences, will always be far more original and interesting than a calculated visual guide to your designs. Portray *you* rather than mimicking or modeling something that's already been done.

Where do you see yourself in ten years?

This is such a daunting question! Once I get past the fear of real life starting to evolve, these questions usually get me very excited! I can't necessarily pinpoint all the details yet, but I see myself connecting the mavens of the fashion industry to women who have been abandoned or abused. I see myself aiding women of all ages and demographics through my work in design. This may look like a multitude of different things, but I know that my personal designs will connect to those in need. I hope I will be far along in my vision to connect high-end fashion and women who are hurting.

On Pins and Needles

Making the decision on what college to attend is a hard choice. Do you like a smaller school or a sprawling campus? Are you looking for something local, or are you willing to move to another city? Tuition and cost of living will vary by school and location. You should also consider whether a particular location will help you to secure a job in the future. For example, in New York you may have more opportunities than in another city to network and apply for fashion internships and jobs.

Look at different schools' course catalogs. Study the types of degrees offered, along with the types of classes you can take. Does the school offer a program that matches your interests and career goals? Are you looking to create fashion or to manage fashion? These are all things to consider when evaluating programs.

SEAL OF APPROVAL

Be sure to find out if the college or art school you are looking at is accredited. Accreditation means the school has met certain quality guidelines. This is extremely important if you plan to attend graduate school in the future. Many graduate schools do not accept degrees from nonaccredited schools. They may require you to take additional classes or complete a new program before admitting you to graduate studies.

The most important thing is to find a school that makes you happy. Visit different schools. Go online and complete virtual tours. Read about their programs. Chat with people who've gone there. Between the school's website and its social media sites, you should be able to answer all of your questions. This is an important decision, so treat it like a research project. It'll be worth it when you find the school that's the perfect fit!

Name: Mary Stephens
Job: Director of fashion design, FIDM

FIDM, HEADQUARTERED IN LOS ANGELES, CALIFORNIA, IS ONE OF THE TOP FASHION SCHOOLS IN THE COUNTRY. THEY HAVE HOSTED THE SHOW *PROJECT RUNWAY* AND WERE FEATURED ON MTV's *THE HILLS*, WHEN STAR LAUREN CONRAD ATTENDED THE SCHOOL. SOME STANDOUT GRADUATES INCLUDE MONIQUE LHUILLIER (CELEBRITY WEDDING-GOWN DESIGNER), PAMELA SKAIST-LEVY (COFOUNDER, JUICY COUTURE), NICK VERREOS (*PROJECT RUNWAY* CONTESTANT, SEASON TWO), AND LEANNE MARSHALL (*PROJECT RUNWAY* WINNER, SEASON FIVE). THE FIDM MUSEUM & GALLERIES HOSTS MAJOR EXHIBITIONS AND HAVE AN EXTENSIVE COSTUME COLLECTION.

What can high school students do to prepare themselves for the application process?
The most important thing young designers can do is become aware of the world around them. They should be inspired by their environment and immerse themselves in culture. Travel; go to museums; see fashion exhibitions; study film, costumes,

and music—every aspect of the world should serve as inspiration and spark creativity.

What qualities are you looking for in candidates?
Design student candidates should be deeply immersed and intellectually engaged in all avenues of design; they must be willing to dedicate their whole life to this pursuit. Other crucial traits of aspiring designers range from creativity and motivation to collaboration skills and a sense of urgency.

What can students expect their first year?
The FIDM Fashion Design program prepares students for careers in fashion design for the apparel industry. In their first year of study, students can expect to take courses in all aspects of fashion design, from technical procedures, such as pattern drafting, draping, sewing, and sketching, to general studies, which includes textile science, computer applications, and the history of fashion.

What are some of the challenges of your program?
The whole program is a challenge! Therefore, a complete dedication to learning the craft and the industry is essential.

How much sewing experience should an applicant have?
No prior sewing experience is required, since that is what a designer learns while in college. However, if a future applicant has the opportunity to take any type of sewing class prior to attending design college, it would be completely helpful.

Why should people interested in fashion design enroll in a formal program versus starting their own fashion business?
The advantage of enrolling in a design program over starting a fashion business without any formal training is the experience that is gained while in school. While there are certainly

exceptions to the rule, most people need two to four years spent pursuing their education, and additional years working in the industry for other established fashion companies, to cultivate their talent and avoid making many costly mistakes.

What advice would you give kids who are showing an interest in fashion?
You must absolutely make fashion your life.

THE MOST EXCITING WEEK IN FASHION

The first fashion week runway show was held in 1943 at the Plaza Hotel in New York City.[3] This weeklong industry event let fashion designers show off their latest clothing designs. Buyers and the media reporters go to these shows to see the newest trends. The main shows are held in New York City, Paris, Milan, and London. The front rows of these shows have become favorite spots for celebrities and music moguls. You can grab your own front-row seat by logging on to the numerous websites that broadcast every designer's show.

Don't be afraid to take time to learn. It's good to work for other people. I worked for others for twenty years. They paid me to learn.

VERA WANG*

28

Learn from the Best

Do you want to do menial tasks, work long hours, and not make money? Then an internship is perfect for you! These sacrifices are worth it if you understand what a great learning opportunity an internship can offer. As a fashion intern, you can work for a designer, in a fashion showroom, or for a magazine. If you keep your eyes and ears open, you will gain a lot of real-world experience you can't get in school.

Fashion interns often work on a lot of different tasks, because they are usually assisting other people. This allows you to see many different areas of the business. You may find your career interests shift after this experience. Many jobs in the fashion industry are behind the scenes, so you may discover some new careers that you didn't know existed.

As an intern, it is important to network with as many people as possible. Volunteer to help out with projects, always arrive on time, and be professional. Many interns are offered full-time paying jobs when their internships are over. Regardless of where your internship leads, you want to make sure you receive great letters of recommendation. Your hard work will pay off for your future.

3

From Design to Runway: Finding Your Niche

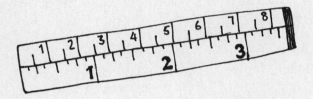

A lot of people know they want to work in fashion, but they don't know where to start. They know they like clothes, but they aren't sure what they want to do. Does this sound familiar? Fashion isn't just glamour and great clothes; it's also a lot of work. Many people who work in the fashion industry work long hours along with evenings and weekends.

If you're going to work so hard, don't you want to find something you love doing? One of the best ways to discover the many opportunities in the fashion industry is with an internship or a job at a retail shop. Both of these experiences expose you to many different careers and teach you some skills along the way. Also, they look great on a college application or résumé. Colleges and future employers are always impressed with people who have experience.

Fashion is something you can study every day. Thousands of fashion blogs are available online, along with fashion magazines and designer's personal websites. Your local mall is a great place for ideas too. Wander into different stores and see how things are displayed. Look at different types of clothes and how they are made.

Put different outfits together. Take pictures of things you like and don't like. This is a great way to get inspired!

Quiz

Your Fashion Personality

Are you having a difficult time pinning down your fashion interest? Take this short quiz to see what areas you might want to dig into.

1. In school I like to take classes in . . .
   a. English
   b. Art
   c. Math
   d. Drama

2. If I were going to help create a movie, I would be . . .
   a. Writing it
   b. Designing the costumes
   c. Building the sets
   d. Acting

3. I would describe myself as . . .
   a. Confident, organized, good at research
   b. Creative, adventurous, risk taking
   c. Precise, focused, good at math
   d. Outgoing, curious, helpful

4. If I could receive one gift, it would be a . . .
   a. Top-of-the-line laptop
   b. Trip to Paris
   c. Sewing machine
   d. Designer handbag

5. When I go with my friends to a school dance, my favorite part is . . .
   a. Taking pics and updating my Facebook page
   b. Altering my dress so it looks like no one else's
   c. Serving on the school decoration committee
   d. Helping everyone shop for dresses

6. My fashion style is . . .
   a. On trend with my classmates'
   b. Unique
   c. Vintage and from thrift stores
   d. On trend with the magazines

7. I would like a career where I can . . .
   a. Report on all of the exciting things happening in fashion
   b. Be creative and express myself
   c. Be part of a team and work behind the scenes
   d. Work with different people

8. When I flip through a fashion magazine, I like to . . .
   a. Look at all of the product advertisements
   b. See the fashion show runway pictures
   c. Compare the quality of how clothes are made
   d. See how outfits are put together and accessorized

9. When working on a group project, I typically . . .
   a. Take notes and ask for everyone's input
   b. Take the lead and direct how the project will go
   c. Pay attention to the details and make sure everything is finished
   d. Make sure the project looks good with great poster boards and props

10. The thing I like most about my favorite clothing store is . . .
   a. They play great music and make it a fun place to shop
   b. They carry a lot of different clothing brands
   c. The clothes are always well made
   d. They follow all the latest trends

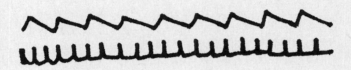

If you answered mostly A's, then you may want to look at having a career in fashion media or marketing. There are so many opportunities, from online blogging or magazine journalism to promoting and selling a designer's fashion line.

If you answered mostly B's, then you're interested in fashion design. You can create your own clothing line or work for a larger design company as part of its creative team.

If you answered mostly C's, then you may want to consider fashion production. This includes careers as patternmaker, cutter, sample sewer, and production manager.

If you answered mostly D's, then you may be interested in working with fashion in a different way. You may consider becoming a model, photographer, or fashion stylist. All of these careers let you meet a lot of different people.

A CHAT WITH FASHION CLUB

Fashion Club was created by FIDM for teens interested in fashion. They offer various college scholarships and contests to their members. Some of their past contests include creating a video on summer fashion trends, sketching clothing designs, and writing an essay on vintage fashion. This is a great source for you to find information on fashion trends, careers, and real-life stories from people working in fashion.

Why was FIDM Fashion Club created?

Fashion Club was created to serve as a resource and as inspiration for high school students interested in pursuing careers in the fashion and design industries.

What kind of resources can be found on FIDM Fashion Club?

Fashion Club attracts an audience of high school students who love fashion and are considering it as a career. To this end, fashionclub.com covers hot fashion trends, beauty tips and trends, DIY videos, celebrity style, and inspiring stories about FIDM alumni and their successes. Contests and scholarship opportunities consistently run on fashionclub.com. There is also a Creative Careers section that offers a career quiz and helpful tips on how to dress for job interviews in the industry. Also, the Fashion Club Blog is updated daily with style trends, industry news, shopping tips, and interviews with FIDM students and alumni, as well as other industry insiders. Regularly scheduled features on the blog include: What's New, What's Hot; FC Link Love; Must-Have Mondays; 5 Fabulous Fashions Under $50; Career Girl Answers; and Ask Fashion Girl.

What is Sketch Class?

Sketch Class is a section on fashionclub.com documenting step-by-step instructions on how to draw the nine-headed fashion figure.

How can Fashion Club help teens prepare for a career in fashion?

Starting or joining an official FIDM Fashion Club is an excellent step toward preparing for a career in fashion. As a member of Fashion Club, you have ample leadership opportunities and chances to network in the fashion industry. Students can produce a fashion show on their high school campus, for example, and invite guest speakers to meetings. Also, there is a constant influx of interviews on the site and the blog in which college students and alumni tell their stories of how they got their first internship or job in the fashion industry. A firsthand account of how people got their start is incredibly inspiring to our readers.

What is a Fashion Club high school club?

FIDM sponsors Fashion Clubs at high schools across the nation. The clubs meet on their respective high school campuses at least twice a month and participate in creative activities, share ideas, learn new things, and explore their interests in the fashion industry—not to mention make new friends. Clubs choose their activities based on their interests, including fashion shows, workshops, field trips, and guest speakers.

How can teens start a Fashion Club at their school?

Any high school student can start an official FIDM Fashion Club. There is no cost. Students visit myfidmfashionclub .com to download the forms and get started. A dedicated Fashion Club staff member mentors the club presidents, walking them through the application process and how to create their business plan.

Make It Work

Have you ever wondered where the whole fashion industry begins? Who comes up with all of the clothing designs, and where are they made? Who decides what's in style? Is it the designers or the magazine editors? How do retail stores know what clothes people are going to buy? Do they have a crystal ball, or is it just a guessing game? Fashion is like every other industry. It involves a process that takes an idea and develops it into something that can be purchased in a store. Here's a brief description on how that happens.

Fashion Design and Production

For the fashion industry to exist, someone must make clothes. A designer starts with an inspiration that later becomes a paper or computerized drawing of a garment. The designer often works with several people who help turn the drawing into an actual piece of clothing. Fabric has to be chosen. Patterns must be cut for various sizes. And someone assembles and sews all of the pieces. Finishing touches like buttons and trim are added at the very end. It's a process that is repeated for every piece of clothing in a designer's collection.

Modeling and Photography

A designer's collection may be shown at a fashion runway show or sold directly to a retail store. Either way, a designer needs a way to show off the designs. This is where models and photographers help so much. A model may wear the designer's clothes in a runway show or pose in a studio for a photographer. All of these photographs are put together into a catalog for the collection. The catalog is needed when meeting with clothing buyers and people interested in reporting on the clothing to the media. The designer works closely with the models and photographers to make sure the pictures tell the right story about the collection.

THE THREE MAIN
CATEGORIES OF FASHION

✂ Haute couture designs are custom-made clothes for a customer. *Haute* refers to something elegant; *couture* refers to sewing. Clothing can be called haute couture only if it meets strict standards. A couture garment typically is sewn by hand. Attention to detail is most important.

✂ Mass-market clothing caters to the everyday customer and is made in large quantities. The clothing follows the fashion trends set by designers and mass media. They use cheaper fabrics and production methods to make the clothing more affordable.

✂ Ready-to-wear clothing is a combination of haute couture and mass-market clothing. Small quantities guarantee quality. These are the clothes that usually walk down the runway during a fashion week.

Fashion Merchandising

Now that the clothing has been made and photographed, it needs to be sold. How do the clothes get from the designer to the person wearing them? Fashion designers sell their clothes to large retail clothing stores, individual boutiques, or directly on their own website. Retail buyers will choose the styles based on what they think their customer will buy. They use different mathematical formulas when deciding how many items to order and how much they will charge a customer. When the clothing arrives, a retailer puts the items on display in their store. Stores usually display their clothing by designer, but some will divide them into different departments.

TRENDING profile

Name: Veronika Scott
Age: 24
Job: Founder and CEO of the Empowerment Project

WHAT STARTED OUT AS A CLASS PROJECT HAS TURNED INTO A PASSION FOR VERONIKA SCOTT. HER ASSIGNMENT WAS TO DESIGN SOMETHING THAT SOLVED A PROBLEM. SHE RECOGNIZED THE HIGH NUMBER OF HOMELESS PEOPLE IN DETROIT AND SET OUT TO DESIGN A SELF-HEATING AND WATERPROOF COAT THAT TRANSFORMS INTO A SLEEPING BAG AT NIGHT. AFTER GRADUATION, SHE CREATED THE NONPROFIT THE EMPOWERMENT PLAN TO CONTINUE MAKING HER SLEEPING BAG COATS. SHE EMPLOYS HOMELESS PEOPLE TO SEW THE COATS IN ORDER TO PROVIDE THEM WITH OPPORTUNITIES TO GET OFF THE STREET. THE SLEEPING BAG COAT HAS ATTRACTED THE ATTENTION OF THE FASHION INDUSTRY, AND SCOTT HAS PLANS TO BEGIN A PROGRAM SO THAT, FOR EVERY COAT PURCHASED, A COAT IS DONATED TO SOMEONE IN NEED. SO FAR, HER ORGANIZATION HAS BEEN ABLE TO KEEP THOUSANDS OF PEOPLE WARM AT NIGHT.

Where did you go to college to study?
I graduated in December 2011 from the College of Creative Studies in Detroit with a bachelor of fine arts in industrial design.

How did the idea of the sleeping bag coat come about?
In the fall of 2010, I was given a class assignment to design something to fill an actual need, and almost immediately recognized how many homeless individuals there are in the city of Detroit. With this in mind, I reached out to a local shelter and

began volunteering, working with a group of homeless individuals. After spending months on this project, I had designed a water-resistant and self-heating jacket that transforms into a sleeping bag. After the semester ended, I realized the idea was much larger than a class project, and that the coat could actually provide warmth and a sense of comfort and independence to those living on the streets. I decided to continue to work with the homeless to create other prototypes and to improve the quality and design of the layout.

What did you discover when designing the coat?
After speaking with a homeless woman one day, I came to realize that the coat is a Band-Aid for a systemic problem and what these individuals really need are jobs. I then went on to hire and train homeless single parents to make the coats. The Empowerment Plan currently employs fifteen seamstresses and is continuing to grow. The Empowerment Plan is unique, as we not only focus on coat production and distribution, but also on the importance of providing educational and vocational opportunities to our women in order to best help them build better lives for themselves and their families.

What kind of career did you originally think you would have after graduation?
Being that I went to school for product design, had internships working with design firms such as Little Tykes, and had discussed that path with my family and professors, I thought I would continue down that same trajectory after graduation. Until I was assigned that class project, I truly thought that I would work for a private design firm, hopefully in New York City, until I could break off and begin doing my own work.

What has been one of the most exciting moments you've had since starting the Empowerment Plan?
Each and every time one of the newer team members goes from living in survival mode (worrying about food, shelter,

and taking care of their children) to becoming the person they always were underneath all of the stress, anger, and worry is truly a beautiful experience for our entire team.

What advice can you give teens who are interested in a fashion career?
Don't be afraid of constructive criticism, of showing your work and being open to receiving honest feedback. Even though there will be times when you will feel like you want to go into a corner and hide your work until you think it is good enough to show someone, be proud of your creativity and your work. Take advantage of those around you with more knowledge and experience—I would not be where I am today without my mentors.

Fashion Media and Marketing

How do people even know a designer exists? They learn about designers and their clothes from the media and marketing. This can happen in many different ways, from an advertisement in a magazine to someone writing an article on a fashion blog. A magazine's back-to-school issue may have an article about the best jeans to buy and then include pictures of the jeans the editor picks, along with the designer's name. This is great for a fashion designer because that person gets free advertising and product endorsement from someone who has researched a lot of brands. People who work in this field have a lot of power. They help create trends, promote designers, and influence people's buying decisions.

The entire process, from a designer's sketch to clothes appearing in stores and magazines, happens several times a year, often fall/winter, spring/summer, and resort collection. By the time a fashion designer's collection is being sold in a store, the designer is already well into working on the next collection. It's a fast-paced industry with very little down time.

HAUTE COUTURE

In the second half of the nineteenth century, a designer named Charles Frederick Worth designed elaborate, one-of-a-kind dresses for French royalty. He was known as the father of haute couture. Many of his dresses can be found at the Costume Institute at the Metropolitan Museum of Art, available for the public to view. Hundreds of hours went into making each gown.

Haute couture is custom-made clothing sewn to a person's precise measurements and the making of it is still practiced today, even though it is a time-consuming process. The garments are usually dresses, which are made from the highest quality luxurious fabrics. Many of them include sequins, rhinestones, or beading, and they are each sewn on by hand. When one of these dresses is completed, it is truly a work of art.

To be considered haute couture, the Chambre Syndicale de la Haute Couture must accredit the design house by meeting the following requirements:

- ✄ The designer must have a workshop in Paris.

- ✄ A minimum of twenty people must work for the designer.

- ✄ The clothing must require more than one fitting, so the clothing fits perfectly.

- ✄ The designer must present at least thirty-five clothing looks in Paris at each season's fashion week.[4]

- ✄ A few well-known haute couture designers are Yves Saint Laurent, Givenchy, Chanel, and Christian Dior.

Tavi Gevinson: The Rookie

It's not hard to admire someone who's on the *Forbes* 30 Under 30 list for changing the world in media. It's even harder not to show admiration when the person is fifteen years old. That's exactly how old Tavi Gevinson was the first time she landed on the list in 2011. She was right back on their list in 2012 and shows no signs of slowing down.

Gevinson was born in Oak Park, Illinois, in 1996. She started the blog *Style Rookie* when she was eleven years old as a way to comment on fashion and show off what she was wearing. Soon she was sitting next to Anna Wintour, *Vogue* editor in chief, in the front row of New York Fashion Week. Many people took notice, and she was interviewed by popular magazines and newspapers. It seemed she was destined to become a great fashion icon.

In 2011 she decided to take her after-school career in a new direction. She decided to bridge her love of fashion with feminism. As she stated in an interview with *New York Magazine*, "I even think that fashion can be a tool of feminism and of self-expression and individuality and empowerment."[5] She founded an online magazine called *Rookie*. This magazine, written mostly by teenage girls, unites and empowers girls through pop culture, fashion, and interviews. In 2012 she published her first book, *Rookie Yearbook One*, which was followed by a second book in 2013.

Tavi Gevinson is proof that you're never too young to begin pursuing your dreams. Her early start has given her a chance to fine-tune her interests.

Name: Isabella Rose Taylor
Age: 12
Job (when not studying!): Fashion designer

Isabella Rose Taylor is only twelve years old but is already making a big name for herself in the fashion and art community. At age three she began painting. By age eleven she was selling out at art gallery shows that displayed her paintings. Her love of art and creating new things led her to fashion design. In 2013 she won the Rising Star Award at Austin Fashion Week for her hippie/grunge collection and began selling clothes on her website. Already a high school graduate, she is attending Austin Community College and is an editor for *Amazing Kids!* magazine. She has been a guest on the *Today Show*, AOL, and *The Steve Harvey Show*. She believes her painting and clothing designs influence each other. As one of the most popular T-shirts from her clothing line states, "If art had legs, it would be fashion."

How did you get started in fashion and designing?
I started painting at a very early age. Around age eight, I was moving into mixed-media work and thought it would be nice to know more about textiles and sewing. I signed up for a sewing camp at that time. I fell in love with fashion during that camp and have been designing clothes ever since.

How do you balance school and work responsibilities?
Sometimes it's really challenging to manage my school and

work responsibilities, so I try to make sure there is flexibility in my daily schedule in order to maintain balance. If something is not working, then I try to change it.

What do you like most about your job?
The best thing about my job is being creative. I love to make things; it's my passion, and I am very grateful to be able to do that.

What is the most challenging thing about your job?
The most challenging aspect for making my clothing line is definitely fabric sourcing. I am on a continual search for fabric. As far as it is being challenging, it's also quite inspiring. Sometimes I get inspired by a fabric I have found for a piece in my collection.

What has been one of the most exciting moments you've had since you started your fashion career?
My most exciting moment was being on national television, but one of the most unexpected thrills has been all the amazing people I have been lucky enough to meet.

Where do you see yourself in ten years?
In ten years I hope to have global recognition of my brand, expand into accessories to complete my looks, and be a mentor to other young girls who are trying to follow their dream.

What advice can you give other kids who are interested in a fashion career?
My advice is my motto, "Blood, sweat, and glitter." You need to have the passion (blood), put in a lot of work (sweat), and be creative (glitter). Perseverance and determination will go a long way toward helping you reach your goals.

FOURTEEN FASHIONABLE FILMS

Documentaries are a great way to learn about your favorite fashion designers and models. You can find many of these films online, on Netflix, or through your cable television provider. Many of these films will also give you a historical perspective on fashion. Watch them for inspiration. They are a great learning tool. See how some of the most famous people in the industry work, think, and live.

1. *Catwalk* (1995)

2. *Yves Saint Laurent–His Life and Times* (2002)

3. *Seamless* (2005)

4. *Marc Jacobs & Louis Vuitton* (2007)

5. *The Secret World of Haute Couture* (2007)

6. *Lagerfeld Confidential* (2007)

7. *Valentino: The Last Emperor* (2008)

8. *The September Issue* (2009)

9. *Picture Me: A Model's Diary* (2009)

10. *A Man's Story* (2010)

11. *Bill Cunningham New York* (2010)

12. *OWN Visionaries: Tom Ford* (2011)

13. *J.Crew & the Man Who Dressed America* (2012)

14. *Once Upon a Time* (2013)

As you start to consider a career in fashion, it's important to think of the many ways you can start educating yourself about the industry. It's a very competitive career, so it's better to start sooner rather than later. Films are a great place to start. All it takes is one amazing idea to point you in the right direction!

4

Creating the Vision: Designer

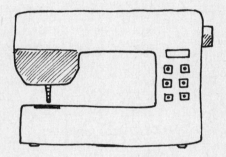

Do you look at pictures from New York Fashion Week or runway shows and imagine your creations walking down the runway? Do you think your name belongs next to those of Elizabeth & James, Marc Jacobs, and Stella McCartney? Becoming a big-time fashion designer is a long shot. It takes a lot of dedication and hard work.

Most people who start their own fashion labels fail. This can happen for a variety of reasons. Many designers are creative but have no idea how to run a business. They may not know how to promote or sell their clothes. Production may be an issue. It's one thing to produce one shirt, but what if a store orders three hundred!? What about creativity? A designer must constantly come up with new ideas and new inspirations.

Does this all sound a little overwhelming? It can be, but that's why it's important to prepare yourself. You can take business and marketing classes. You can work as an intern for a designer. You can get a job working on a design team for a larger fashion house. Information is everywhere if you just look!

Designer vs. Stylist:
Are They the Same Thing?

Some people find these job titles a little confusing, since many people do both jobs.

A fashion designer develops the inspiration for the clothing and gets them made. This is usually done without one particular individual or specific occasion in mind. The designer is all about creating the garment and having it produced.

A fashion stylist selects clothing based on who is going to be wearing it and what that person will be doing while wearing the outfit. A stylist may dress a celebrity for a red-carpet event or party. A singer may have a stylist put together outfits for music videos. Stylists often work with advertisers and magazines for photo shoots. They don't design or create clothing. They put together whole looks by pulling together clothing, accessories, and sometimes hair and makeup from various sources.

Where Do Designers Find Their Inspiration?

A short answer to that question is that designers find inspiration everywhere. Here is a list of some of the most common places:

✂ Art museums and galleries

✂ Comic books and anime

✂ Current fashion magazines

✂ History books

✂ Pop music

✂ Nature

✂ Studying different cultures

✂ Travel

✂ Vintage clothing shops

✂ Vintage fashion magazines

✂ Watching teenagers and how they put outfits together

Activity

Create an Inspiration Board

One of the ways to start on your design career is to create an inspiration board. It's a collection of things that inspire you to create.

1. Buy a large corkboard or poster board to display your findings.

2. Collect pictures from magazines, album covers, and art books.

3. Add fabric swatches, ribbon clippings, and buttons.

4. Add some more! Anything that stimulates your imagination should go on your board. The wonderful thing is there aren't any rules.

5. Edit. This means you want to start looking for common themes and grouping items together, so your collection tells a story. Maybe you've noticed certain colors keep showing up. Maybe most of your

inspiration comes from a certain time period or from a particular region.

6. Hang your completed inspiration board in your workspace. You should be able to see it from where you do your sketching. Every time you feel a little stumped, look at your inspiration board for a boost of creativity!

. . . .

Create your own individual style. I'm not interested in the girl who walks into my office in a head-to-toe label look that's straight off the runway. I'm interested in a girl who puts herself together in an original way.

ANNA WINTOUR[6]

Technology and Fashion Design

Do you like to sketch out a design using pencil and paper? Or would you prefer a more high-tech approach? Many designers are now turning to technology when creating their designs. Computer-aided design (CAD) software is used to draw clothing, try different colors, and change the dimensions of the model. This software is great because all of the measurements are precise, so if you are making clothes in different sizes, there are fewer mistakes. A virtual model lets you experiment and make changes quickly. It's perfect for the designer who isn't great at sketching because the software does the drawing for you. You can take a class on how to use CAD software. Many of the programs include tutorials.

Digital drawing pads let you sketch out a design with a stylus. You can try out different colors and textures on your design and print out your pictures when you are done. The show *Project Runway* gives their contestants digital drawing pads to sketch out their outfits. If you have access to a tablet computer or touchscreen device, you can start practicing. Either use your finger to draw or pick up a stylus from an office supply store or anywhere that sells computers. You'll have fun watching your ideas come to life.

The How-Tos of Design

Sketch your inspiration. The designing process begins with an inspiration. This is where creating an inspiration board comes in handy! A designer creates a sketch for each item of clothing in the collection. The designer must consider what type of fabric to use and choose the colors and patterns. Trimmings such as zippers, ruffles, buttons, and bows are often used to add details to the clothes.

Turn the drawing into a reality. A dress form is a three-dimensional mannequin used to give the designer a realistic view of a garment. Draping fabric on a form, the designer makes adjustments to the sketches and creates a pattern. The fabric is marked and pinned, so the designer sees how the fabric will be cut and sewn and can make more adjustments if necessary. Once the fabric is removed from the dress form, a paper pattern is created, using the markings as a guide. The paper pattern is used to guide the cutting of the fabric and prepare it for sewing. After the garment is sewn, it is put back on the dress form, so the designer can make any changes or alterations to the look.

Learn to sew. Sewing skills are a must and something you can start practicing right now. It's one thing to be able to draw, but being able to make those designs come to life is a whole other skill.

Look again for inspiration. The designing process never ends, so you must be creative. Attention to detail will give you an edge, because people are always looking for high-quality items. As a fashion designer, you have endless possibilities on what you can create, which is why so many people are drawn to this profession.

Name: Andy Truong
Age: 17
Job (when not studying!): Fashion designer

SEVENTEEN-YEAR OLD ANDY TRUONG IS A SELF-TAUGHT FASHION DESIGNER IN SYDNEY, AUSTRALIA. AT THE AGE OF SIX, HE STARTED HELPING HIS MOTHER SEW BUTTONS ON GARMENTS. FROM THERE HE DEVELOPED A LOVE FOR FASHION AND DESIGN. HE TAUGHT HIMSELF TO SEW BY WATCHING YOUTUBE VIDEOS AND READING ON THE INTERNET. IN ELEMENTARY SCHOOL HE MADE SCARVES AND IPOD COVERS TO SELL TO HIS FRIENDS. NOW, AS A BUSY HIGH SCHOOL STUDENT, HE WORKS TWO JOBS TO HELP PAY FOR PUTTING HIS FASHION COLLECTIONS TOGETHER. IN 2011 HE LAUNCHED HIS FIRST FASHION COLLECTION, AND IN 2013 HE SHOWED HIS COLLECTION AT THE MELBOURNE SPRING FASHION WEEK. HIS HARD WORK HAS PAID OFF, AND HE IS WELL ON HIS WAY TO FULFILLING HIS DREAMS.

When did you discover your love for fashion and designing?

I discovered my love for fashion when I was a young child. My love for fashion and design was ignited when my dreams started to become reality when I was twelve years old.

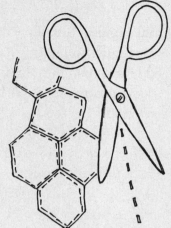

How do you balance school and work responsibilities?

I try to accomplish everything in a timely manner, but I'm not perfect. I don't get everything I want done in the timeframe I'd like. I devote my time to my designs every Wednesday afternoon, and any spare time when my homework is complete. It's a full schedule, but I love it.

What do you like most about your job?

Making my dreams a reality and helping my clients' dreams come true too.

What is the most challenging thing about your job?

The most challenging thing is finding the funds for my elaborate dreams. Sometimes I might have this amazing image of the final piece of design in my head, made with feathers and silk lace and diamonds and all these fancy materials; then I realize that it costs too much. I have to downsize the design to an affordable cost without sacrificing my original look.

What has been one of the most exciting moments you've had since starting your fashion career?

It's always exciting to hear one of my designs have been sold and then spotting my designs on the internet. Another exciting moment is when I check my bank account and see my hard-earned money coming through!

Where do you see yourself in ten years?

Hopefully in ten years, my brand will be an established brand in Australia, and I'll start thinking of going global. In five years, I hope to be showing in New York and then another five years later in Paris.

What advice can you give other kids who are interested in a fashion career?

The best tip I can give is to not be afraid of doing things. If I had let my fears for showcasing at Melbourne Spring Fashion Week win, then I would be nowhere now. Aim high and if you fall, brush yourself off and go again. Everyone gets knocked down, but if you pull yourself together, that makes you better than the rest. I can't remember how many times I was told that my designs would not sell in the boutiques because the designs were "too young" or "didn't fit with store," but I didn't stop. I continued designing what I'm good at, and now I have found stockists, and my designs are selling.

Different Types of Fashion Designers

So, you know you want to be a fashion designer—right? Do you know what type of fashion designer you want to be? Do you know about the many options for designing? Did you know there was more than one type? Fashion covers everything from the shoes on your feet to your clothes to the hat on your head. Fashion is worn by real people on the street and by characters in movies and onstage. If you go to the beach, you can see fashion in swimsuits, hats, sunglasses, flip-flops, and bags, and if you go to college campuses and office buildings, you see it in the outfits people wear to class, work, and events. What items would you like to design? Maybe the following career descriptions will help to inspire you.

Clothing Designer

Clothing designers create all of the wonderful clothes in our closets. Their job is to create or anticipate trends so that people want to buy their clothes. Many designers like to choose a specialty, whether it's making clothes for men, women, kids, or events, such as weddings. Specializing helps them to be more recognizable. For example, Quiksilver is known for making surfwear. Other designers, like Ralph Lauren, like to dabble in everything. His brand designs clothes for every occasion. He has sportswear, formal wear, and swimsuits for men, women, and children. Designers have a lot of choices when creating a brand.

In 2013, Rad Hourani became the first fashion designer to be admitted to the La Chambre Syndicale de La Haute Couture for unisex clothing. The clothing line, called RAD by Rad Hourani, launched in 2007, and Hourani was mentored by the president of Christian Dior, Sidney Toledano. His designs can be worn by both men and women. In addition to focusing on quality craftsmanship, Hourani likes his clothes to be functional. One of his blazers can be worn fourteen different ways, from a backpack to a skirt.

Costume Designer

Costume designers create the look of each character in a film or play. Their first job is to read the script and interpret how each actor should look. This includes clothing, accessories, wigs, and makeup. The designer must research the fashion from the time period and place in which the story takes place. Props and how the set is designed will help reinforce the look the designer is trying to create.

It is important for a costume designer to be a team player. The director will have a vision for the performance, and the costumes need to reflect those ideas. Set designers and the lighting department need to be consulted so the costumes complement the rest of the production. After the designer's costume sketches are approved by the director and production crew members, the designer must create the clothing. Many costumes are created from altering or changing clothing that already exists. The rest are made from scratch. Designers must keep in mind which characters will be onstage together and what the set will look like. They don't want the characters to be wearing similar colors or to clash with the set.

If you want to work in costume design, then you must be good with details. You not only have to keep track of all the different costumes that need to be created, but you also need to know when characters are scheduled to have costume changes. You have to be good at working with many different people with many different ideas. Budgets and deadlines are strict in this line of work. If this is something that interests you, then you should consider helping out with your school's performances. You'll see firsthand that it's fun when the characters come to life on stage.

Footwear Designer

Footwear designers help us dress our feet. Their job is to give people what they want to wear, whether they are designing for men, women, or children. Designers must consider construction, comfort, and materials. Everyone wears different types of shoes, depending on the occasion. You wouldn't want to wear high heels to kick a soccer ball! Shoes vary as much as clothing. They can be athletic, formal, sandals, boots, or casual.

Footwear designers work alone or with a small team. The design process starts with designers researching trends. Shoes must complement what is happening in fashion. After a designer has an idea, they create a sketch of the shoe. If the designer is working for a client, the client must approve the sketch and any subsequent changes. CAD software helps to translate a sketch into a realistic-looking picture and lets the designer try different colors on the design. Many times a prototype of the shoe will be built, so a client can see an exact model of the shoe. A specification sheet is then created for manufacturing. This gives the shoe manufacturer exact instructions on how to make the shoe. After the shoes are made, they are shipped off to our favorite stores for people to buy.

To be a successful footwear designer, you have to be interested in everything happening in fashion. Shoes and accessories must go with the clothing people are wearing. An understanding of foot anatomy is necessary if you want your shoes to be feel good on people's feet. More and more people are demanding their shoes be stylish and comfortable. If you are interested in shoes, then you should start learning about famous shoe designers. Many of them started their career because they saw a gap in the industry that was not being fulfilled.

About half my designs are controlled fantasy, 15 percent are total madness, and the rest are bread-and-butter designs.

MANOLO BLAHNIK[*]

Accessory Designer

A great accessory can change a boring outfit into something exciting. Accessory designers create jewelry, belts, scarves, hats, and handbags. These are the finishing touches that make each person's clothing look unique. If you go to a school where kids have school uniforms, you'll notice how each kid uses accessories to look unique. Whether they're shoelaces, belts, bracelets, purses, or hair bows, accessories let a person show off their personal style.

To be a great accessory designer, you must have inspiration. Accessories don't follow seasonal trends as much as clothing and footwear, so an accessory designer has more flexibility with what they can create. A sketch shows the basic idea of the accessory. Details and functionality are added next. These may be clasps, buckles, zippers, or handbag pockets. A prototype of the design allows the designer to examine the look and quality of the product. After any changes are made, the product specifications are sent to manufacturing, so the accessory can be made in large quantities for resale.

Many accessory designers have a signature look, so their designs are immediately recognizable. For example, a designer's initials or a brand logo may be used on every design. Every type of accessory is constructed differently, so an accessory designer usually specializes in one type of accessory. For example, a jewelry designer must know how to work with metals and stones. If accessory design interests you, then you should try creating different types of accessories. Or just experiment with how you use accessories to change the way you look. The possibilities seem endless!

Name: Whitney Pozgay
Job: Fashion designer

WHAT DO YOU GET WHEN YOU COMBINE A TOUCH OF WHIMSY WITH A FEMININE DESIGN? YOU GET WHITNEY POZGAY'S CLOTHING LINE WHIT. AFTER GRADUATING FROM THE UNIVERSITY OF TEXAS AT AUSTIN WITH A DEGREE IN THEATER AND A CONCENTRATION IN COSTUME DESIGN, SHE MOVED TO NEW YORK. IN 2007 SHE WAS THE WOMEN'S WEAR DESIGNER FOR STEVEN ALAN AND LAUNCHED HIS BRAND FOR URBAN OUTFITTER'S, LARK & WOLFF. BY 2010 SHE WAS READY TO MAKE A NAME FOR HERSELF AND LAUNCHED HER OWN CLOTHING LINE CALLED WHIT. SHE'S

BEEN FEATURED IN *WOMEN'S WEAR DAILY*, *LUCKY*, AND *ELLE*. HER CLOTHING COLLABORATION WITH ANTHROPOLOGIE EARNED HER INSTANT PRAISE FOR HER FOCUS ON THE PETITE BODY FRAME.

When did you discover your love for fashion and designing?

I have always been interested in fashion, but I went to school for costume design and theater. I started interning in fashion during my summers and, after moving to New York, became a receptionist at Kate Spade while taking night classes at Parsons and FIT to bridge the gap in my formal education.

How was the transition from working for someone else to starting your own clothing line?

There is a certain freedom that you take for granted when working for someone else. While I had a lot of different responsibilities in my previous roles, I was able to focus mainly on design. When you have your own business, you have to deal with difficult questions that aren't necessarily fun or creative. You have to be very regimented about organizing your time so you have the energy to also be creative.

Where do you find inspiration for your fashion design?

I am always looking and absorbing, but I try to develop a space in my mind each season for a unique story to take root. It can have its origin in a real place, or maybe it's imaginary, and I populate it with ideas and images that I can then draw

from. When that story is vivid, the design process becomes organic, but you have to be dedicated to enriching that landscape because it usually only gives back what you put in.

What do you like most about having your own line?
What I love the most is also the most terrifying aspect. You are in complete control of where you choose to aim: it is your vision, your passion, your creative self. It is a wonderful feeling, but it can also leave you very exposed, knowing you will be judged for what you put out in the world.

What is the most challenging thing about having your own line?
There are so many moving parts it can make your head spin. Dealing with that reality while you try to grow creatively can at times be a heavy burden. I think the challenge is being at ease with decisions that have no clear resolution. You must grow accustomed to wading through murky water at times.

Is there anything that has shocked you about this business?
I think the industry has a bad reputation of being cutthroat, and that is rarely the case in my experience. When we started WHIT, I was really nervous to reach out to stores and editors, but you have to be a squeaky wheel. I was shocked by how receptive and open to meeting people were once I stopped being afraid to reach out.

What advice can you give kids who are interested in a fashion career?
I cannot stress enough how important it is to work for other designers before starting a new line. Learning the process and the business of fashion is imperative. Also, while this business might look really glamorous from the outside, it takes a lot of hard work, and you have to be really scrappy. Just loving fashion is not enough. There is a lot of manual labor and long

hours that go into each collection. If it is truly someone's passion, it is worth it, but you have to be willing to put in the time. Most important, always be sketching and writing down ideas. Try to feed your creative reference pool with new visual experiences as much as possible.

Are You Thinking About Starting Your Own Design Business?

Do you think you have what it takes to strike out on your own? Are you interested in becoming your own boss? Are you ready to deal with accountants, lawyers, manufacturers, and suppliers? Here are some things you need to think about before starting:

Research and create a road map. A solid business plan shows you are serious about your business. It's where you state your company's purpose and why your company is different.

Know your customer. What specific type of customer are you designing for? It's important to understand your customers and how they want to dress. Consider your price points as well and what type of store your customers shop.

Budget, budget, budget. Where's the money coming from to start your new business? You need much more than just the supplies to design and sew your garments. You will have fees for office equipment, business licenses, marketing, and staff. Putting a budget together for creating your design samples helps you to determine how much you can spend on the other items.

Create samples and a catalog. One of the first steps to selling your designs is having clothing samples to show store buyers. After you have your samples, take pictures of your designs. You can create a catalog to give store buyers that includes pictures and pricing.

Network like crazy. It's much easier to create a business if you have help. Start by first building your network of necessities. This might include an accountant, a lawyer, a factory for creating your clothes, photographers, and models. You also want to have a group of people who believe in you and will help to promote your business.

Assess your strengths and weaknesses. With any type of business, it's important to know what you're good at and where you need help. Does the idea of talking to a store owner about selling your designs make you nervous? Then maybe you want to hire a salesperson to help you out.

Consider a partner. Many of the most famous fashion designers have partners. This is a great way to divide up the workload and have someone to share ideas with. Look for someone who has different skills from you and who has a great work ethic, just like you have.

CONTESTS AND CLUBS

Contests and clubs are a fun way to gain experience and test your skills. Small and large events are happening in every major city. Contact your local sewing stores, libraries, and community colleges and ask if they are sponsoring any events. If you are having difficulty finding anything locally, then it's time to look online. Do an internet search on the name of your city and "fashion design contests or clubs." If this doesn't turn up anything, then try searching "teen fashion design contests or clubs" and see what national events are taking place.

Bethany Mota: YouTube Sensation[7]

How does a bullied teenager become one of the most popular girls on the internet? She starts a fashion and beauty YouTube channel! This is exactly what Bethany Mota did five years ago at the age of thirteen. Now that she's eighteen, she has over 6 million YouTube subscribers, 1.25 million Twitter followers, and 2.5 million fans on Instagram. Her videos feature tips on fashion, makeup, and hairstyles. Her down-to-earth conversational style has made her a favorite for teen girls. Recently, she was asked to collaborate and design a clothing and jewelry line for Aeropostale retail stores. The collection includes over eighty items. A nationwide tour of their stores has her fans flocking to their local malls to meet her. She's been featured on the *Today Show* and *Entertainment Tonight*, and in *Teen Vogue*.

Where Can You Sell Your Clothes?

There are several different ways you can sell your designs. No matter which route you choose, make sure you have the resources to produce and deliver the clothes on time. First impressions are very important when dealing with new businesses.

Department stores: This is the most difficult way to sell your clothes as a new designer. Store buyers receive lots of requests for meetings and can pick up a limited number of new clothing lines every year.

Local boutiques: This is a great entry point. Many times you can set up an appointment with the store owner to show your designs. This is a great way to receive feedback about your clothes, whether the stores purchase them or not.

Trunk shows: Stores like to do trunk shows for new designers because they don't have to buy the clothes up front and resell them. It's a great way to test the waters on new designs.

Website: You can set up a store on the internet to sell your clothes. You control all aspects of the business. Be prepared to spend a lot of time getting the word out about your website.

Online marketplaces: Websites like etsy.com help you sell your designs. You pay them a small fee to list your items with a picture on their website. Sites like this usually provide you with tools and assistance on how to sell online.

PROJECT RUNWAY FOR KIDS AND TEENS

In 2013, the Queens Library in New York City held its own version of *Project Runway* for kids and teens. There were ten teams of one designer and one model each. The designer had to take old men's clothing and turn it into fashion for women to wear. The winners were designer Alyssa Sadofsky (age sixteen) and model Corine Houngninou (age ten). Their prize was to attend the taping of the season eleven finale for the *Project Runway* show. They met some of the judges, designers, and models. It was an experience they will never forget.

5

Putting the Whole Look Together: Stylist

Do you have the urge to make over every person you meet? Can you visualize how to use different hairstyles, makeup, clothes, and accessories to change a person's appearance? That's great! Because stylists have to be good at styling people from head to toe. They are responsible for every aspect of a client's look. Every detail counts when it comes to being a stylist.

The idea of revamping someone's wardrobe may sound fun, but it's a lot of work too. It's not just about shopping and dressing people.

THE TOP SEVEN SKILLS EVERY GREAT STYLIST HAS

Business skills: You manage a lot of money or store credit for the clothing and accessories you need. Income can be unsteady if you're working freelance, so good budgeting skills come in handy. Consider taking an accounting class if it's offered at your school, or start using a budget to manage your own finances.

Networking skills: A great relationship with designers, retail stores, photographers, models, makeup artists, and hairstylists helps you when it comes to providing options for your clients. Sometimes you don't have a lot of time to pull something together for a client, so it's great to have contacts who can help you out. If you work in a retail store, you can help people pick out clothes, which tests your skills at styling–and may earn you new clients.

Time-management skills: You have to be able to manage many different projects at one time. Some may be long-term assignments, and others may come up with short notice.

Emotional skills: Styling is not a job for wimps. You have to be able to accept criticism, rejection, and, even if the client is happy, the possibility of not being thanked or of not receiving recognition. Also, everyone you work with (including your clients) may offer opinions on how you should do things as a stylist. You should always listen to what others have to say because that's how you learn. Never be afraid to try something new!

Trendspotting skills: It's your job to know what's in style now and what will be in style later. Your clients expect you to use this information when choosing their clothes.

Self-motivation: In the beginning of your career, clients won't be coming to you. You will be searching for them. It takes a lot of work to earn new clients, but it will be worth it when they start giving your name out to their friends.

Good instincts: It's important to know how to match an outfit to fit a personality. For example, someone quirky like singer Katy Perry wouldn't wear the same thing as Jennifer Aniston, who likes casual looks, to a formal event.

Name: Nick Wooster
Job: Creative advisor

CHANCES ARE THAT IF YOU SEARCH ONLINE FOR THE NAME
NICK WOOSTER, YOU'LL FIND THOUSANDS OF IMAGES FOR THIS
STYLE ICON. NOT ONLY IS HE A FAVORITE OF STREET PHOTOG-
RAPHERS AND BLOGGERS, HE'S REDEFINING MEN'S FASHION ONE
COLLABORATION AT A TIME. RAISED IN SALINA, KANSAS, HE
WENT TO WORK AT JOSEPH P. ROTH AND SONS CLOTHIERS,
THE NICEST CLOTHING STORE IN TOWN, AT AGE SIXTEEN. AFTER
EARNING A COLLEGE DEGREE IN JOURNALISM AND ADVERTIS-
ING FROM THE UNIVERSITY OF KANSAS, HE MOVED TO NEW
YORK CITY. WITH A FASHION CAREER SPANNING OVER THIRTY-
FIVE YEARS, HE'S WORKED AS A DESIGN DIRECTOR FOR RALPH
LAUREN, A FASHION DIRECTOR AT NEIMAN MARCUS AND AT
BERGDORF GOODMAN, AND A SENIOR VICE PRESIDENT OF TREND
AND DESIGN AT JCPENNEY. HE'S WORN MANY HATS IN THE
FASHION INDUSTRY AND HAS USED EACH CREATIVE EXPERIENCE
TO LAUNCH A NEW OPPORTUNITY.

When did you discover your love for fashion?

I got started in fashion because my mom said if I wanted nicer
clothes, I'd have to earn the money to buy them myself, so I
figured out a way to get a job at the nicest clothing store in
town. I started working there when I was sixteen
years old. It never occurred to me that there
was a fashion business, just the clothing business. I wanted nice clothes—ergo I worked
in the nicest clothing store.

How has the industry changed in the last thirty years?
The industry has completely changed. Wholesale companies
have consolidated. Major department stores are now down
to about four, so with the supply and the demand shrunken
down, everything about the business has changed. It's the era
of the big conglomerates. In the old days, brands and designers sold to stores. Now everyone is in the retail business. In
addition to the consolidation at the wholesale and retail levels,
brands who used to only sell to third parties have become
retailers themselves. Hence the rise of the vertical retailer.
Gucci, Prada, and J.Crew all have their own stores.

What do you like most about your job?
Clothes. The only reason I'm interested in the fashion industry is purely selfish. I'm only interested in clothes, like when
I'm working with product, working with designers, creating
product, or buying product. That's the point. Otherwise, it's
just paperwork.

What is the most challenging part of your job?
Uncertainty. The uncertainty of the next step or what the
newest job will be. When you consult with a number of companies, it's like people in the entertainment industry. You are
only as good as your last project. You never know what the
next is going to be. In terms of challenges on a project, I
think it's personalities that are always the most challenging.
The fashion industry is full of big personalities.

**What has been one of the most exciting moments you
have had since starting in this industry?**
The actual moment was when I became the men's fashion
director for Neiman Marcus and Bergdorf Goodman. It was
the job that I always wanted, and it took twenty-five years
[since I first started working toward it] for it to happen, but it
happened. I think that's the message: don't quit before the mir-
acle. You have to work for things, and I think it's a common

misperception that things come easily to people. In the end, regardless of the industry, persistence pays off handsomely. In my case, that's what happened.

How has social media changed the fashion industry?
Social media has changed the fashion industry the way color television has changed the entertainment industry. It's yet another way to communicate ideas and a vision. A lot has been said, good and bad, about social media and the internet, but at the end of the day, television didn't kill the radio. It just changed the way it's consumed. I think it's the same with social media. It's just another way for more people to have information quickly. The business is relearning and rewiring itself to adapt to this reality.

What advice would you give kids who are interested in a career in fashion?
Start now! By that I mean, the two things I require before I would even meet with someone is an active social media presence and experience working in retail. You have to be involved in retail, in my opinion, in order to be successful. Whether you're a designer, a brand, another vertical, it doesn't matter. It ultimately comes down to customers. The best idea isn't a good idea if it doesn't sell. The quicker you can understand that fashion is a business, the better off you'll be, regardless of the field that is of interest to you.

Careers in Styling

Stylists need a lot of inspiration. Think of all the different clothes, shoes, and jewelry you see at the shopping mall. Now imagine having to pick from all of those items—and even more exciting, for a photo shoot. Stylists do this every day. They are excellent at looking through thousands of options to find that one perfect thing. Details are important if you want to survive as a stylist. You must be organized and always prepared. If styling is the gig for you, then here are some opportunities you might want to consider.

Editorial Stylist

Editorial stylists often work for fashion magazines. They usually attend runway shows, meet with designers, and help choose the fashion themes for that month's publication. After a theme is chosen, then a location has to be selected, models hired, travel plans made, and a photographer chosen. Not to mention all the choices around the dozens of clothing options, along with hats, sunglasses, jewelry, and shoes. An editorial stylist will often work with an assistant and some interns who help to gather everything for a photo shoot. The team has to overprepare for every photo shoot in case something goes wrong. For example, if it starts raining, the stylist will need to be prepared to add a raincoat and boots to the outfit instead of canceling the plans. It pays to be flexible in this job!

Celebrity or Corporate Stylist

A celebrity or corporate stylist works for an individual. This includes putting together head-to-toe looks for red-carpet events, photo shoots, and company functions. This type of stylist is often called at the last minute because of a party or big event a client is attending. If you are going to be this type of stylist, you must have access to a lot of clothing options on short notice. Sometimes a client will hire a stylist to choose a daily wardrobe. That professional will buy everything from jeans, T-shirts, and evening wear to jewelry, purses, and shoes. A stylist helps the client create a unique clothing image.

Video Stylist

Being a video stylist allows you to be part of different types of productions. You help models, actors, and singers choose wardrobes for commercials, music videos, and films. Wardrobe selection is usually only part of this job. Video stylists help hire staff and oversee models, makeup artists, hair stylists, and photographers during the taping. The hours are often long on filming days, but it's exciting to see your work come alive on film!

Retail Stylist

A retail store has a lot of styling opportunities. Somebody has to put together the displays in every department. Some stores create window displays that are works of art. The Macy's store in New York City has one of the most famous window displays in the world during the winter holidays. A personal shopper styles clients based on the clothing, shoes, and accessories available in the store where they work. They look for clothing based on the person's needs and body type. Opportunities in retail stores vary based on the size of the store. Good customer service is key to being successful in this job.

Whatever your interests may be, there's a styling opportunity for you. Stylists are used everywhere from television and live theater to music videos and personal shopping. A stylist's job is not always glamorous. You may spend a lot of time hiring models, finding locations, tracking down accessories, and leaving messages for designers. Some days are just spent unpacking, packing, and shipping out clothes. It's a big job that often involves a lot of people. For a stylist, it's all about helping clients to look their best!

It's a new era in fashion—there are no rules. It's all about the individual and personal style, wearing high-end, low-end, classic labels, and up-and-coming designers all together.

ALEXANDER MCQUEEN[8]

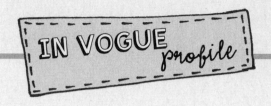
IN VOGUE profile

Name: Lauren Messiah
Job: Personal stylist

WHAT DO YOU DO IF YOU HAVE A HEAD FOR BUSINESS AND PAS-
SION FOR FASHION? IF YOU'RE LAUREN MESSIAH, YOU BECOME A
PERSONAL STYLIST. AFTER EARNING HER BFA IN FASHION DESIGN
FROM VIRGINIA COMMONWEALTH UNIVERSITY, SHE WORKED
FOR THE ONLINE MEDIA CORPORATION AOL AND IN HER FREE
TIME DEVELOPED A VIRTUAL STYLING BLOG. SHE COMPLETED
THE STYLING PROGRAM AT SCHOOL OF STYLE AND A TRAIN-
ING PROGRAM WITH STACY LONDON OF TLC'S *WHAT NOT TO
WEAR*. NOW SHE IS A PERSONAL STYLIST, FASHION EXPERT, AND
ON-AIR FASHION ADVISOR IN LOS ANGELES, CALIFORNIA. SHE
IS THE PRESIDENT AT THE SCHOOL OF STYLE. MAJOR RETAILERS
LIKE MARSHALLS, TARGET, AND EBAY HAVE USED HER STYL-
ING EXPERTISE. HER CLIENTS HAVE WALKED RED CARPETS AND
ROCKED THE MTV MUSIC AWARDS.

When did you discover your love for fashion?
I've known since I was a little girl that I wanted to work in
fashion. I started out by getting my BFA in fashion design
at Virginia Commonwealth University's School of the Arts.
After graduating I got that age-old reality check that just
because you earn a degree doesn't mean you'll be the next
Marc Jacobs. I moved back home and got a retail job at Betsey
Johnson. Since I desperately wanted to move out of my par-
ent's house, I left that job and got a position as an executive
assistant at AOL. Not exactly living the dream, but I took
advantage of my downtime (those lulls in between scheduling
appointments and fetching coffee) and started a blog where I

styled people online. My blog opened a lot of doors for me. A powerful executive at AOL saw my blog and transferred me to Los Angeles to work on a new fashion-related project. I quickly entered the online fashion world, but after five or so years, I wanted more. I wanted to style real people instead of online people. So I quit my fancy internet job and struck out on my own as a stylist. I haven't looked back since.

What do you like most about your job?
I'm about to sound really corny but being able to help people and truly change their lives simply by doing what I love to do. Most of the women I style are real women (noncelebrities), and shopping and getting dressed are a real chore. Whether it is due to the lack of time, insecurities, or feeling like they don't deserve to look their best, they literally need someone to come in and help them with their style. Having a personal stylist doesn't have to be some frivolous and material thing; it is really a tool to help women look and feel their best.

What was the most challenging part about starting your business?
The biggest challenge for me was in the beginning. I had to make some major life changes in order to pursue my career as a stylist. Working freelance as opposed to having a 9:00 AM to 5:00 PM job meant no more regular paychecks, no health insurance, moving into a cheaper apartment (with a room-mate), and cutting out nonessential purchases. I went from making six figures to living off unemployment, and from having employees to working as someone's intern. Of course I would totally do it all over again, but at the time it was a bit of a challenge.

What has been one of the most exciting moments you've had since you started styling?
I've been really fortunate to have such a multifaceted career that affords me so many exciting opportunities. The moment

that stands out the most was my partnership with Westfield, Australia. Westfield Mall was doing a campaign where they had four stylists representing different parts of the world. I was chosen to represent the USA. I was flown to London to shoot three television commercials that aired in Australia. This was my first time ever on camera and my first time out of the country. Because of this once-in-a-lifetime opportunity, I was featured in *Marie Claire* and *Grazia*. Talk about a pinch-me moment, especially since this happened so early in my career.

How do you balance your various roles as a stylist, blogger, brand ambassador, and writer?
My life is one big juggling act; sometimes I don't even know how I do it. I am very type A and hyperorganized so keeping notebooks filled with to-do lists and ideas keeps me sane. I also have calendars everywhere with all of my deadlines and due dates. I am a workaholic, so I force myself to take breaks by scheduling "me time" into my calendar (told you I was type A). Pilates in the morning; walks with my dog, Yohji; and the occasional Netflix binge keep me sane.

What advice would you give kids who are interested in fashion styling and writing?
The advice I always give to my students is to stay devoted to your dream because this isn't an overnight deal. Patience is key. Be a sponge and learn from the people who came before you by interning for and assisting them. There is a huge misconception about stylists; people seem to think that Rachel Zoe and June Ambrose, for example, became who they are overnight. They worked hard for years before getting those A-list clients, reality shows, book deals, and the like. Slow down—your big break is coming. Just enjoy the ride and learn everything you can along the way.

Know How to Pick Fashion that Flatters

Styling is all about making people look their very best. The first step to doing this is knowing your clients and their body types. Different body shapes look better in different types of clothes. You want to make sure you emphasize a person's best features. It's more important to wear flattering clothes than to wear what's trendy. The stylist's job is to find a balance between what's in style and what looks best on a client. The following are the five most common body shapes.

Apple Body Shape

An apple-shaped body means a person is wider through the stomach and bust and narrower through the hips. Stylists use clothes to create a smaller waist. At the same time, they try to draw attention to their clients' best body parts, like their great legs! Some good clothing styles for this shape are wrap dresses, wide-leg jeans, and structured jackets. Celebrities who look amazing with this body shape are Kate Winslet, Jennifer Hudson, and Drew Barrymore.

Pear Body Shape

A pear-shaped (or triangle-shaped) body is wider at the hips than the shoulders. This is accented by a tiny waist and small arms. Stylists use clothes to show off the upper body and downplay the lower body. A shirt with a lot of details matched with a pair of straight-leg jeans will draw a person's eye up. A maxidress is a great way to show off a small waist and shoulders. Celebrities who know how to rock this body shape are Kim Kardashian, Jennifer Lopez, Beyoncé, and Kelly Clarkson.

Rectangular Body Shape

Someone with a rectangular body has shoulders and hips that are almost the same width. This often creates an athletic look. A stylist's job is to create curves by defining the waist with clothing. A pair of jeans with button-back pockets or a pencil skirt soften up this body shape. A belted sweater cinches in the waist and makes it look smaller. Celebrities who know how to accentuate this look are Cameron Diaz, Natalie Portman, and Gwen Stefani.

Hourglass Body Shape

An hourglass body shape has hips the same width as the bust. This highly coveted body shape looks curvy because of the person's small waist. Stylists play up this body shape with clothes that follow the natural curves of the body. They avoid anything that looks too boxy. Belted jackets and dresses show off the waist and show off the body's curves. Celebrities who claim this shape are Halle Berry, Jessica Biel, and Marilyn Monroe.

Inverted Triangle Body Shape

An inverted triangle body (or wedge shape) features prominent shoulders. They are broader than the hips and can make a person look strong and athletic. Stylists will be looking for clothes that add more volume to their client's hips to balance out the shoulders. Cargo pants or jeans with textured fabric are a good choice. They will want to keep the shoulder lines on shirts simple. No structured jackets or shoulder pads. Celebrity beauties with this body type include Cindy Crawford, Jennifer Garner, and Giselle Bündchen.

 *Style is a way to say who you are without having to speak.*

RACHEL ZOE[9]

Brad Goreski: Larger than Life

If you are interested in becoming a fashion stylist, then you've probably heard of Brad Goreski. His larger-than-life personality landed him an Old Navy commercial and his own show on Bravo called *It's a Brad, Brad World*. He is known for his own personal style, along with dressing some of the hottest celebrities. Some of his A-list clients include: Minka Kelly, Jessica Alba, Stacy Keibler, and Demi Moore.

Born in 1977 in Ontario, Canada, Goreski loved looking through *Vogue* magazine as a teenager. He attended the University of Southern California and graduated with an art history degree. After internships with *Vogue* and *W* magazine, he got an assistant job with the West Coast division of *Vogue*. He became a household name when he began working for famous celebrity stylist Rachel Zoe and appeared on her reality television show, *The Rachel Zoe Project*.

In 2011 he decided to strike out on his own and open his own business. His television show documented his business's slow start, when he was styling out of his home's garage, to his rise as a celebrity stylist working out of a beautiful office building. His approach to styling is to solve clients' clothing issues. "One thing I have learned in this industry is that you cannot be part of the problem; you have to be part of the solution," Goreski stated.[10] His enthusiasm for his work keeps his list of clients growing. Look this guy up if you're interested in reading his star-studded styling tips!

Tools of the Trade

One of your jobs as a stylist is to always be prepared. You never know if you're going to need to nip, tuck, or brush when you're getting someone ready for a big event. The pros keep a bag of tools with them at all times to handle big and small emergencies. Here are some of their favorites:

- ✂ Double-sided tape to hold garments in place

- ✂ Scissors to cut any hanging threads

- ✂ Camera to take pictures of the completed look

- ✂ Baby powder to help with tight shoes

- ✂ Lint rollers to clean garments

- ✂ Pins to fix a garment

- ✂ Clips, used in photo shoots to give clothes the illusion of a perfect fit

- ✂ Stain remover to hide any marks

- ✂ Assorted undergarments for a perfect and smooth fit

- ✂ Plenty of backup clothes in case something goes wrong!

6

A Cut Above the Rest: Production

Do you like working in a team environment? Are you good with numbers? Maybe your favorite tools are a pencil, ruler, and scissors? That's fantastic! Because a lot of fashion designers can use someone like you. Designers need a lot of help when it comes to making their sketches a reality: actual clothing. At large fashion houses, it takes a team of people to draw, measure, cut, and sew the clothing.

When a designer sells their garments to a store, they will need to make it available in several different sizes. The production team must change all of the measurements, so no matter what the size, it still looks like the same garment. These changes to the pattern affect how the fabric will be cut and sewn. One garment may come in several sizes, colors, and types of fabrics. All of this information must be put together into a set of very clear instructions.

Most designers have their clothing made in factories. It is important for the designer's production team to have detailed plans to give the factory for each garment. Most clothing is made overseas, so it may be too late to correct any mistakes that might be made, and the designer has to decide whether to send it to the stores with the mistake or on to an outlet store. If a pocket is put in the wrong place or a shirt is made too short, it can make the garment look cheap. Designers don't want to put their names on items that aren't made well. It is the job of people working in production to make sure the design looks as fabulous in real life as it does on paper. It is one of the most important jobs in the industry.

From Sketch to Garment

How does a sketch become an actual piece of clothing that someone can wear? Sometimes the fashion designer will make a pattern and then sew the design, producing the piece from start to finish. Designers with more resources often have several production workers who can help them get their designs to manufacturing. These people are experts at their job and are often good with details. Let's look briefly at the steps following a designer's work, which involve a patternmaker, cutter, and sample sewer, three members of the production team.

1. The first stop to getting a design produced is to have a pattern made. A patternmaker's job is to take the designer's sketch and break it down into pieces. They make paper outlines of each piece and create a list of instructions on how they should be sewn together. The pattern is marked where every button, zipper, or pocket will be located. Patternmakers need to be knowledgeable about computers, so they can reproduce the pattern in different sizes using CAD software.

2. After a pattern is created, it is passed over to the cutter. Fabric is expensive! The cutter's job is to maximize the use of a designer's fabric. This person draws outlines of the pattern onto the fabric and cuts the fabric by hand. The cutter must

know how to work with different types of fabric. For example, a fabric with stripes needs to be cut in a way that allows everything to be lined up when the pieces are sewn together. After the fabric is cut, it is bundled together and stored by size and color.

3. The next step is to sew everything together. A sample sewer follows the directions on the pattern to sew the new design. This gives the designer a chance to see if there are any problems with the design or pattern before sending it off to be mass produced.

4. Once the sample is approved, the garment moves on to manufacturing. This is the last stop before clothing is sent out to be sold in stores.

A good use for me is to let me go away with my sewing machine and come back with some really new stuff.

BETSEY JOHNSON*

Nicolas Caito: Transforming One Dimension into Three

Who do designers call when they have complicated fashion sketches they want translated into patterns? Chances are they call Nicolas Caito. *Elle* has called him "New York's most in-demand patternmaker."[11] He takes one-dimensional sketches and turns them

into three-dimensional prototypes. By draping mus-
lin on a mannequin, he plays with the fabric until
it looks like the designer's vision. He uses this as his
blueprint to create the paper pattern, which allows the
clothing item to be produced.

Born in France, Caito didn't think he'd follow in
the footsteps of his grandparents, who were tailors
in Sicily. He began his college studies in business but
discovered his true passion after visiting his uncle's
tailoring studio. At age twenty-one, he started interning for the designer Lanvin, where he stayed for seven
years. From there he spent eighteen months at Hermès
before he decided to move to the United States.[12]

His move to New York City launched him into the
American fashion scene. He opened his own atelier,
which is a patternmaking workshop. He works with
many different fashion designers and private clients.
Anyone can walk into his shop with a design idea and
get his help. If someone wants a unique party gown
or wedding dress, Caito can help that person come up
with something that's one of a kind.

Patternmaking Tools

Patternmakers have a very special job. They are in charge of
providing the blueprint for how a garment should be created. A
pattern is the template essential for re-creating the same garment
over and over again and always getting the same results. It provides
all of the measurements and instructions for turning a sketch into
a beautiful piece of clothing. Since all of the numbers must be
precise, patternmakers have special tools they use to figure exact
measurements.

- ✂ Fabric scissors

- ✂ French curve (tool shaped into a curve and used to mark armholes and necklines)

- ✂ Hip curve ruler (twenty-four-inch curved ruler used to create hiplines on skirts and pants)

- ✂ L-square ruler (used to transfer people's measurements to a flat pattern)

- ✂ Paper

- ✂ Patternmaking paper

- ✂ Pencils and fabric pens

- ✂ Notcher (hole punch used to mark seams when the pattern is completed)

- ✂ Straight pins

- ✂ Tape measure

- ✂ Tracing paper

- ✂ Tracing wheel

- ✂ Yard stick

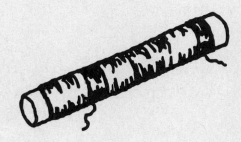

One of my greatest talents is recognizing talent in others and giving them the forum to shine.

TORY BURCH[*]

Seamstress

A person who makes a living sewing is called a seamstress. Sewing is a skill-based profession that you can learn while doing the work. You can start by signing up for some classes at your local craft or sewing store and then practicing at home. As a seamstress, you will be expected to know how to sew hems, apply zippers and buttons, and make alterations. Knowing how to read a pattern is extremely important, since this is your set of instructions on how to sew the garment.

A lot of learning happens when you work with different fabrics. Some fabrics stretch or wrinkle when they are sewn together or washed. An experienced seamstress knows how to construct the garment so it holds up well and looks good when it is worn. The attention to detail makes the difference between a garment that looks high-end and one that looks shoddy.

Like mechanics who use tools to fix cars, seamstresses have their own sets of tools. They may have large-scale sewing machines, embroidery machines, dressmaker forms, and a variety of sewing accessories. Seamstresses can work in department stores doing alterations. They may work for fashion designers in a studio or in a larger factory.

Names: Erin Albin and Megan Oser
Job: Designers and shop owners

In 2005 sisters Erin and Megan started their accessory design business on a dining room table in a small apartment. They sold their handmade bags and accessories on the weekends at the Portland Saturday Market craft fair. What started as a part-time business became a full-time affair when the sisters opened up their shop, Appetite, where they create textiles, sew their designs, and sell directly to their customers. They produce two annual collections, which include bags and home accessories.

When did you discover your love for fashion and sewing?

Our mother and our grandmother always sewed our clothing and things for the house, so we learned to sew and craft at an early age. We would design and sew fashions for our Barbie dolls, sew Christmas gifts for friends and family, and eventually we made clothing, blankets, pillows, and curtains for ourselves.

Where do you find your inspiration?

When we began designing nine years ago, we found most of our patterns and colors came directly from nature. As technology has evolved in our lives, we find that much of our print design and colorways are influenced by what we see globally. The internet and Instagram have become great informants of inspiration, from showing us what our peers are interested in to allowing us to view an entire archive of vintage textiles. Each season we pick a theme and try to develop patterns based around it. We have also found that growing up in the Southwest has had a big impression on our style, especially in our shop.

How did your business get started?

Erin visited Portland, Oregon, as a teenager and while in the city attended the locally famous Portland Saturday Market. That visit made a huge impression on her, as she saw so many people selling their handcrafted items in one venue. Shortly after moving to Portland after college, Erin became a regular vendor at the Portland Saturday Market.

Was it exciting to open your own retail space?

We had a long-time aspiration of opening a retail space, and it moved from dream status to a reality in a quick thirty-five days in the spring of 2012. The right space became available, and it pushed us to make our dream happen more quickly than we thought we were ready for. It was a bit daunting, but we were too busy and committed to have any time to worry about it.

What are some effective things you've done to grow your business?

We've worked hard on branding ourselves, and while we still grow and change, we remain recognizable to our clientele. We did and still do participate in many local street fairs and craft fairs to promote our business. We try to keep the prices at the store and in our wholesale line at a reasonable cost, especially with our vintage merchandise. We get feedback that our customers appreciate this, and it has created many regular clients for us.

What are some of the biggest challenges in this business?

We've found it hard separating work time from personal time. Your business is like a child, and it needs constant attention and nurturing as it grows. It's always on our minds and in our conversations. We're still figuring out how to create a balance between the two.

What has been one of the most exciting moments you've had since starting in this industry?
For us it's the little daily things that are very small yet so meaningful, like seeing a bag we've made on the arm of a lady walking down the street or a loyal customer opening her Appetite bag from six years ago and showing us her array of Appetite accessories that she has in that bag and getting a new piece to add to her collection. It's so gratifying that people love what we do and continue to support us.

Where do you see your business in ten years?
In ten years, we hope to be less physically involved in the actual production of the bags, accessories, and homewares. We would like to remain a small company with few employees and keep our production local.

What advice would you give kids who are aspiring designers?
It is important to start with strong ideas for what you want to design and how you want to achieve that, but it is also important to be open to changing in ways you may not have imagined. Also, do internships and collaborations often. The things you learn from other designers, makers, and businesspeople will help inform your design and expose you to more aspects of business.

Production Manager

While a designer makes creative decisions, the production manager makes sure they happen. The production manager handles all of the details that allow a designer to focus on the designing. The manager is often the point of contact with suppliers of fabrics, trimmings, and packaging. Communication with the factories producing the designer's clothing allows the manager to make design changes and to check on delivery dates. A good background in accounting and math will come in handy for this job. You may be asked to keep track of costs, inventory, and sales.

If you are interested in this career, then you are in luck. Production managers are in high demand. You can earn a college degree in production management at most fashion colleges. In this program you take classes in problem solving, computer software programs, and manufacturing.

Production Assistant

Before working your way up to manager, you may need to complete an internship or take a job as a production assistant. This entry-level job allows you to gain experience while working with the production manager. You may have your own job duties or help the production manager complete projects. Either way, it is a great training ground for understanding the full process of turning a sketch into a garment that will be sold at a store.

Textile Designer

A textile designer uses the latest technology to create printed, woven, and knitted products. This designer does this by first understanding how the fabric will be used. For example, fabric used for a shirt may not work as pants. A textile designer must create fabrics based on the weight, strength, and style needed for the garments they will become.

Once the type of textile has been chosen, then the designing begins! Designs on fabric can be created with hand painting, embroidery, or textile printing. The size of the pattern is influenced by how the fabric will be used. Textile printing can be done using a variety of methods including:

Screen printing: a process where paint is applied directly to the fabric by dragging it across the fabric held by a frame

Roller printing: a process where a machine creates a design on the fabric; the machine starts with white fabric and every roller prints a new color or part of the pattern until it is complete

Block printing: the slow process of stamping a design onto fabric that will be available only on high-end products

Digital printing: a process that transforms designs created with graphics software like Photoshop or Illustrator, using special inks based on what type of fabric the printer is filled with

A degree in art and design for textiles, with accreditation, can be found at over three hundred schools in the United States. In these programs, you are introduced to different ways to create fabric, how to use graphic design software, and sketching and design. In most programs, you build a portfolio to show future employers.

Name: Gina Kim
Job: Textile designer

PRINTFRESH IS A TEXTILE DESIGN STUDIO IN PHILADELPHIA, PENNSYLVANIA, THAT CREATES FABRIC PRINTS AND EMBEL-LISHMENTS. CLOTHING DESIGNERS BUY THEIR PRINTS OR

COLLABORATE WITH TEXTILE DESIGNERS TO CREATE SOMETHING THEY NEED. THE STUDIO'S AMAZING CLIENT LIST INCLUDES J.CREW, POTTERY BARN, H&M, URBAN OUTFITTERS, ZARA, ABERCROMBIE & FITCH, AND THE GAP. THE DESIGNERS CREATE APPROXIMATELY EIGHTY NEW DESIGNS A WEEK AND SELL AT LEAST ONE PATTERN TO OVER THREE HUNDRED BRANDS PER YEAR. THAT IS ONE CREATIVE—AND PRODUCTIVE—COMPANY!

What is a typical workday like?

During a typical workday, I will create between three and four designs. The approaches to these designs vary; some designs require painting or drawing things intensively by hand, while others can be created solely on the computer using Photoshop or Illustrator. I love my job because every single day, without a doubt, I get to be creative. There really isn't a typical day at Printfresh since projects always vary, and I can come up with new approaches each time. My day is as good as I choose to make it! I also take a bit of time each day between designs to browse the internet and look at websites or blogs that inspire me.

How do you begin working on a project?

After a project has been pitched to me by my art director, the next step is to search for additional inspiration and reference images. I also like to plan out possible layouts by drawing little thumbnails of my designs, which really helps me from getting off track during the design process. If I'm feeling stuck with searching the web for inspiration, I can take a quick trip downstairs to our amazing vintage archive and get lost in a huge collection of vintage prints and embellishments. Not only is it inspiring, but it's extremely fun. Printfresh also has a huge image library put together by the designers that we can always reference if we need images for anything. Sometimes, just looking through the images is a great reminder of the vast amount of possibilities each design opportunity holds. With all of these tools right at my fingertips, it's easy to get in the mood to design something fresh and new.

Where does the inspiration come from?

Inspiration for a design can come from many different places. While looking at prints on the runway and in retail stores can be very inspiring, it's so much fun to look in unexpected places to find new perspectives and techniques for designing prints. I love looking at art blogs like Colossal to see what artists around the world are doing and what materials they are using, and I also love looking at sites like *National Geographic*'s to see different patterns and color combinations that occur in nature. I've found that it's very easy for me to get too locked into one way of thinking about designing prints for clothing, and I end up running out of ideas, fast. It's important to always keep looking and seeing different things. If I see something and I am drawn to it, I try to figure out why, whether it be the colors, the material quality, or the simplicity of the motif, and when I get a chance, I'll apply it to a design I'm working on, as long as it doesn't detract from the original idea.

How do you make your samples?

I work in Adobe Photoshop and sometimes Adobe Illustrator to create my prints. I may create paintings or drawings by hand and then scan them into the computer, or in some cases I will complete a print design from start to finish on the computer using a tablet. Once the designs are finalized, I test the colors by digitally printing small portions of my designs onto fabric. Designs intended for graphic T-shirts are printed on different types of jersey fabric, and all-over prints are printed on different silks. This testing process is repeated until the colors are approved, and then the full, completed designs are sent to be printed and steamed by the production team. For some pieces, namely children's graphic T-shirts, I really like to add some extra embellishments on them after they are printed. This can include foiling, beading, glitter, or even some fabric embellishments. I have the freedom to find new ways to accent the graphics and bring a whole new dimension to a design for the future client. This is one of my favorite aspects of my job because it brings out the kid in me and feels less like work and more like play.

What is the collaboration process between you and clothing designers?
I usually work very independently when I am designing, but Printfresh is great because all the designers sit together in an open floor plan. I always turn to my coworkers and ask them their opinion on something I'm working on or if they have any ideas for where I can look for more inspiration. Getting feedback and hearing other perspectives for a project are invaluable in this industry, and I get to take advantage of those things every single day surrounded by extremely talented artists. If I am stuck on a specific painting style that I know one of the other designers does really well, I ask them to teach me, and vice versa. We are all each other's teachers and students. It's amazing how much I've learned from my coworkers.

What kind of skills does a textile designer need?
Before I got to Printfresh, I majored in textile design at Rhode Island School of Design, which I think was a huge asset when entering this industry. I think every textile print designer must be experienced with drawing and painting and have an understanding of patterning. In this increasingly digital world, it is also important to be able to work digitally as much as it

is to work by hand. A good sense of color is also crucial when designing for textiles.

What advice would you offer kids who are interested in this profession?

My coworkers and I all have different backgrounds when it comes to what we studied in school, so there is no perfect formula for getting a textile design job. There are people at Printfresh who've studied graphic design, textile design, illustration, and fashion design. Besides the obvious advice to take classes that would help you build the skills to land a textile design job, my advice would be to look, draw, and paint as much as possible. You can never see too many things. Decide what you like, what you don't like, and figure out why. Be open to new ideas and always try to find a new way to approach a project. Remind yourself that since fashion is constantly evolving, your skills must also constantly evolve. Don't ever become complacent. When applying for a textile design job, your personality and portfolio are the most important, in my opinion, so make sure you have a strong portfolio that represents your strengths and personal style.

Be fluid. Treat each project differently. Be water, man. The best style is no style. Because styles can be figured out. And when you have no style, they can't figure you out.

JAY-Z[13]

7

Reaching the Masses: Public Relations and Retail

Are you interested in fashion and business? Then you may want to consider a career in fashion merchandising or marketing. A fashion designer's ultimate goal is to sell clothing, and working in public relations (PR) or retail, you may be just the person to do it.

- ✀ A person working in fashion marketing or public relations has the job of getting people interested in a designer's clothing or accessories.

- ✀ The fashion buyer brings items into the store to be sold.

- ✀ The fashion merchandiser figures out the best way for a store to sell the clothes.

- ✀ The sales associates help customers and ring up the sales.

Every person is an important part of the process.

And this is an easy industry to start getting experience in at a young age. Apply for a job at a department store or boutique. Working on a showroom floor with customers is an invaluable experience for any career in fashion.

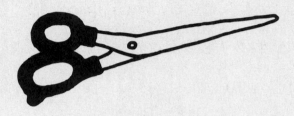

Fashion Marketing and Public Relations

Do you love the idea of helping a designer build up a company? Would you enjoy calling magazines and talking to editors and fashion journalists about a designer's clothes? Does the idea of planning a fashion show sound exciting? If so, you may enjoy a job in public relations. In public relations, you are responsible for putting your designer's clothing out in front of customers. You might do this by convincing a magazine editor to publish a review of the designer's work, planning an event to show the clothes, or contacting stylists about dressing their clients in your designer's clothing. This job involves a lot of networking, so you want to be good at building relationships.

A great way to prepare for a career in public relations is to treat yourself like a client. Build a positive and professional online reputation across your social media accounts (Tumblr, Twitter, Instagram, etc.). Think before you post something! Avoid sharing overly personal information. Remember, you are building your most important brand: you!

Someone who works in public relations must have strong writing skills. You will often be asked to write press releases and marketing strategies. This is why many people who are interested in this career earn a college degree in journalism, English, or marketing.

Of course, nothing can replace real-world work experience, so an internship is also highly recommended.

Name: Crosby Noricks
Job: Fashion public relations

WHEN DESIGNERS NEED SOMEONE TO HELP LAUNCH A BRAND, THEY CALL CROSBY NORICKS. SHE IS AN EXPERT WHEN IT COMES TO PUBLIC RELATIONS AND TEACHING PEOPLE HOW TO PROMOTE THEMSELVES. WITH A MASTER'S DEGREE IN MASS COMMUNICATION AND MEDIA STUDIES FROM SAN DIEGO STATE UNIVERSITY, SHE HAS TAUGHT COURSES AT FIDM AND WAS THE DIRECTOR OF SOCIAL MEDIA FOR RED DOOR INTERACTIVE. RECENTLY, SHE HAS DEDICATED HERSELF FULL-TIME TO HER GROWING WEBSITE, PRCOUTURE.COM. ALWAYS IN DEMAND, SHE HAS COVERED MERCEDES-BENZ FASHION WEEK AND HAS WORKED WITH *TEEN VOGUE*. HER BOOK, *READY TO LAUNCH: THE PR COUTURE GUIDE TO BREAKING INTO FASHION PR*, GIVES AN INSIDER'S LOOK INTO THE BUSINESS. IT'S EASY TO SEE WHY iMEDIA PLACED HER ON ITS 2012 25 INTERNET MARKETING LEADERS AND INNOVATORS LIST.

Why did you start PR Couture?

I created PR Couture in response to the lack of information available online about fashion public relations. I wanted to provide a place where current and aspiring fashion publicists could come to learn important industry news, be inspired by strategies and tips, and see their profession celebrated. The site has since evolved to also include a job board, fashion PR agency directory, media contact lists, and more.

In what ways do social media and public relations intersect?

Public relations is responsible for managing the relationship between a company and its public (basically anyone who already does—or should—have an interest in what's going on). To that end, the communication that happens between a company and its social media community can be seen as the domain of public relations. Social media is a rich mix of customer service and engagement, as well as PR and marketing campaigns. Social media should be a consideration in any PR campaign.

What social media sites are the most successful for public relation campaigns?

It very much varies, and the platforms are continually changing. Generally, the platform where a company either has the highest number of followers or the most engaged number of followers is best. However, taking advantage of a new or emerging social media platform can also be an effective strategy because of the newness of the platform. In fact, being the first fashion brand to execute a campaign on a new platform can become news in and of itself!

What is the most challenging part of your job?

As a business owner, I find that the most challenging part of my job is the fact that the success or failure of PR Couture is 100 percent my responsibility. Each decision I make, and the results of those decisions—from the books I write to the ways I monetize the site—have a direct impact on how well the business does and, by extension, how good I feel about what I am putting out into the world.

What has been the most exciting moment you've had since you got started in fashion public relations?

It's been seven years since I started, so I will pick three really big moments. The first was being sponsored by Microsoft to attend fashion week in New York. We attended several shows, and at the end of the Diane von Furstenberg show—when she walked out—this somewhat mythical figure for much of my life was right there. That was a magic moment. The second moment was the night of my book launch party. Just taking a moment to celebrate what I had written with friends, coworkers, and readers (not to mention the edible glitter and cupcakes) made it an evening I'll never forget. The third moment happened just this year, when I started my first Monday morning having left my big-time, director-level job to focus on PR Couture full-time. Sitting down to my computer that sunny morning, with a big cup of coffee and a great playlist, was a very important day for me.

Where do you see yourself in ten years?
Much like where I am today, except with a cool little family and a much bigger closet.

What advice would you give kids aspiring to work in fashion PR?
Learn as much as you can about the industry by taking advantage of all the great fashion industry publications available to you online. Start a blog; write about the brands you love. Grab friends and spend the weekend doing crazy photo shoots. Learn photography; learn to edit those photos. Take classes in coding and graphic design. Don't wait for permission—just start your own thing.

TYPES OF EVENTS PR PLANS

Product launches are when a new clothing or accessory collection needs to be introduced to the world and usually a party is thrown.

Fashion shows are some of the most important moments in public relations. For a designer's show, PR professionals prepare guest lists and seating charts, talk to the press, and help with other show details. Sometimes a public relations company will spend almost an entire year planning for one fifteen-minute runway show!

In-store events are a way for public relations professionals to get a product into their customers' hands quickly. These events may include a fashion show, free makeovers, or product giveaways. PR people have to think of creative ways to encourage shoppers into the store.

Public appearances are very helpful if a designer is launching something new, for example, a clothing designer decides to come out with a jewelry line. Customers love to meet the people who design what they love to wear, and it's a way for people to get excited about new products.

Casting Director

Did you ever wonder how models are chosen for a fashion runway show? Casting directors are able to take thousands of models and narrow them down to just a few during a casting session. They look for models who can convey the mood and theme for a particular designer's show. It takes more than just a pretty face! They must have the right attitude, body type, and walk. In addition to runway shows, casting directors often match models to photographers and stylists. This may be for fashion editorials in magazines or in advertising campaigns. During a single afternoon casting session, a casting director may see hundreds of models.

Name: James Scully
Job: Casting director

JAMES SCULLY IS NO ROOKIE WHEN IT COMES TO THE FASHION INDUSTRY. HOW CAN YOU BE WHEN YOU'VE WORKED WITH DESIGNERS LIKE CAROLINA HERRERA, TOM FORD, STELLA MCCARTNEY, DEREK LAM, OSCAR DE LA RENTA, AND JASON WU? SCULLY IS A CASTING DIRECTOR WHO IS IN CHARGE OF CASTING MODELS FOR FASHION DESIGNERS' RUNWAY SHOWS. THIS INCLUDES SCHEDULING THE MODELS, NEGOTIATING THEIR CONTRACTS, AND PRESENTING THEM TO THE DESIGNERS. IN COLLEGE HE HELPED OUT BACKSTAGE AT BERGDORF GOODMAN'S RUNWAY SHOWS. IN 1993 HE CAST HIS FIRST RUNWAY SHOW FOR DESIGNER TODD OLDHAM. HE IS AN ADVOCATE FOR LAWS PROTECTING CHILD MODELS AND IS CONSIDERED AN INDUSTRY EXPERT.

How would you describe your current job?
I am a casting director. I am hired by designers and potential advertising clients to choose models (male and female) to represent their brands through fashion shows, advertising, as well as eCommerce projects.

How did you get started in fashion?
Up until about the mid '90s, all public relation companies that represented fashion also produced shows for their clients.

I started at Kevin Krier in 1993 in show production. Todd Oldham was my first client, which at the time was one of the big shows in New York. It was supermodel central. Very shortly afterward, Tom Ford took over Gucci and hired us to do production and that was the client that made my reputation for having created "the Gucci Girl." I left show production to do a stint as the bookings editor of *Harper's Bazaar* in 1999. Then was rehired in 2001 by Tom to work again on Gucci and Yves Saint Laurent, which started my freelance career.

How do you choose models for a show?

I intentionally and creatively choose clients that all have very different points of view, so I can create casts for their individual images. When I look at models, I know the minute I see them if they may work for one client, several, or in some cases all of them. For example, for J.Crew I'm looking for wholesome good looks and a sparkling personality. For Tom Ford I'm looking for someone who looks rich, expensive, exotic, and exudes sexual aura and aspiration. For Carolina Herrera I'm looking for a model that looks refined, monied, ladylike, and has a somewhat icy confidence. Stella McCartney wants a model she believes she could hang out with, so personality, life experience, and confidence are almost second to looks, no young girls here. This is about a woman who is in touch with her girly side, but there is nothing girly about her. She's naturally sexy. So this is the initial process I use when I begin my castings.

What do you like most about your job?

I enjoy the creativity of being able to assemble a cast of characters for each show and create an image that goes out, so when people see the shows I work on, they know exactly who the Herrera, J.Crew, Stella McCartney, Tom Ford woman or man is. My clients know exactly what they are looking to project, and it's very exciting to present them with someone that makes them excited to put in their shows. And the travel that goes with the job. Through this job, I've had the chance to travel the globe, which was the reason I came into fashion in the first place.

What is the biggest challenge in your job?

There are so many, but at the moment the two biggest are celebrities who have taken the majority of work from models and have shrunken the market for experienced talent and money jobs, therefore making the business less aspirational and less attractive for men and women to seek it out as a career. Also, the speed of the business today and the addition of resort and pre-fall collections and internet lookbooks and eCommerce have now basically turned what was a seasonal two-times-a-year job into a full-time all-year job. The constant amount of work and shorter times in which to produce and create work burns out the careers of models in half the time, and constantly searching for turnover of new talent has become a bit overwhelming.

What has been one of the most exciting moments you've had since starting in this industry?

I would have to say it was the now-iconic Gucci satin shirt show for fall 1995. It was a very depressing, minimalist time in fashion. The Gulf War had taken the joy out of fashion ostentation, and the athletic bodies of the '80s were out, and Jil Sanders's show style was pretty much adapted by many designers, taking the theater out of shows, and fashion was very covered up and nonsexual at the time. I think we all knew there was the beginning of something special backstage, but as soon as Amber Valleta walked out, people started really applauding, then for Shalom Harlow in the next outfit, and Kate Moss in the third. We knew halfway through that show the collection was a hit, and the tide had turned in fashion at that moment and something new started right there. The electricity in the room at that time and the powerful feeling backstage that a real fashion moment had happened is something I've been fortunate to experience many times in my career, although with the speed and the access people have to fashion these days, they are fewer. It will be interesting to see how fashion adapts to the Information Age, as it is harder to create surprise with the amount of information people want and how fast they need it these days.

What advice would you give kids who aspire to become models?
Stay in school. My belief is that this business is no place for anyone under eighteen. You need life experience and a really strong sense of yourself, as a lot of this business is based on rejection, even if you are Kate Moss, and it can really mess with your perception of yourself. In the thirty years I have done this, other than Christy Turlington and Kate Moss, no one male or female has walked through an agency door and become an instant success. From Linda Evangelista and Naomi Campbell to current stars Candice Swanepoel and Karlie Kloss, all of the greatest models spent years getting to where they are now, so never expect this to be a place where a career happens overnight.

Fashion Buyer

Don't you wish you could get paid to go shopping? Well, you can! Being a fashion buyer is much more complicated than shopping for yourself, but you do have a bigger budget. You have to consider the store you are buying for and what your target customer wants to buy. If you are lucky, you will attend fashion runway events to see the latest trends. Your job is to predict what clothes will be popular and buy them for your store. Buyers read market reports, talk to customers, and track what sells well in their stores.

Sometimes the buying choices are made based on cost, availability, and selection. The delivery dates are really important because a store never wants to be stuck without enough clothes to sell. The job can be very exciting! You may be the first person to discover a new designer and feature those clothes in your store. If you have a head for numbers and love to follow fashion trends, then you're already ahead of the game.

FASHION WEEK FOR A BUYER

During a big-city fashion week, a buyer's day can start at 8:00 AM and go until 11:00 PM. Buyers are expected to attend several runway shows and presentations every day. During the shows, they take notes on trends they are spotting and items they are interested in for their stores. They pass these notes on to assistants who start putting together information and photographs of the garments. All of this information has to be compared to a client store's sales from last season. If the store sold a lot of long dresses, then the buyer may want to make sure to be on the lookout for long dresses. If coats sold poorly, then maybe the buyer will consider purchasing fewer coats. The buyer takes this information into consideration before making buying decisions. By the end of the fashion week, the buyer has made several purchasing decisions.

PATTERN

A Day in the Life of a Fashion Buyer

8:00–10:00 AM	Read emails and listen to phone messages. Take care of any paperwork, messages, or phone calls from the previous day.
10:00 AM–NOON	Go to appointments with clothing vendors or visit stores and speak to customers and sales associates about the store.
1:00–3:00 PM	Analyze buying reports to see what is and isn't selling in the stores.
3:00–4:00 PM	Look at clothing samples and inspect clothes for quality.
4:00–5:00 PM	Have a meeting with marketing, assistant buyers, and accounting.
5:00–6:00 PM	Clean up desk and prepare schedule for the next day.

The Gap's approach to fashion is "to be current not trendy; classic but not conservative; youthful but not young; reliable but not predictable, and above all, authentically American."

STEVE SUNNUCKS, GAP GLOBAL PRESIDENT[14]

Retail Merchandiser

As a retail merchandiser, you are responsible for creating a wonderful customer experience in your store. The fashion buyer may select the clothes, but you select how the clothes will be displayed once they arrive at the store. Behind the scenes, you'll be making big decisions. You keep an eye out for bestsellers and slow sellers, and work with marketing to create promotions based on this information. Your job is to help the store sell as many clothes as possible. Planning is key in this job. Decisions you make about how many clothing lines to buy will affect the store for several months. You use computer reports based on prior sales to help you. A store's location may affect these decisions too. A department store in Kansas will probably sell more coats and heavy sweaters than its location in Florida. Understanding your customers and the business side of selling clothes is the main job of a successful retail merchandiser.

WHAT'S THE DIFFERENCE?

Many people have a difficult time understanding the difference between a fashion buyer and a retail merchandiser. This is understandable, considering some smaller stores use one person to do both jobs. The buyer and merchandiser work closely together. The easiest way to keep the two jobs straight is to remember that the buyer picks out the clothes, while the merchandiser figures out the best way to sell them. Here are a few other differences to keep in mind:

Fashion Buyer

✄ Looks for upcoming trends

Fashion Buyer (continued)

- ✂ Scopes out new designers for the store

- ✂ Chooses what clothes to buy from the designers the store currently displays

- ✂ Maintains relationships with designers and their associates

- ✂ Orders merchandise

Retail Merchandiser

- ✂ Analyzes sales numbers

- ✂ Knows what customers are shopping for

- ✂ Rearranges the store layout to increase sales

- ✂ Plans markdowns to sell older inventory

- ✂ Tracks inventory

Tom's Shoes: Shoes for One and All[15]

Blake Mycoskie started Tom's Shoes in 2006 after a trip to Argentina opened his eyes to the number of children without shoes. His company donates one pair of shoes for every pair of shoes sold, otherwise known as the "One for One" program. So far they have donated over 10 million pairs of shoes. The business has grown to include eyewear, which uses the same formula for giving: one pair of glasses sold provides eye care to one needy person who struggles with eye impairment! In 2013, Tom's extended their goodwill by launching Tom's Marketplace, which features products from over thirty small companies who donate a portion of their sales to social causes. A customer visiting the website can search by product, by region, or by the type of cause the company represents. Tom's Marketplace has made sure it has something for everyone. You can find anything from jewelry to earphones to dinnerware. They even sell hammocks! Their goal is to become a one-stop shop for both men and women, and to raise awareness for various charities and causes.

It's not about a demographic, it's not about a specific person, it's not about a specific style—it's about having your own style and liking a piece. That's a great entry point [into fashion public relations and retail] for a lot of people.

JENNA LYON, CREATIVE DIRECTOR AT J.CREW[16]

Sales Associate

As a fashion sales associate, you are the first person shoppers meet when they walk into a clothing store. Your job is to help customers find what they need and to increase the store's sales. This includes financial transactions such as ringing up sales on a cash register, setting up store credit accounts, and figuring sales prices. Sales associates work with clothing inventory and help keep track of the new clothing coming into the store. In most stores, they are in charge of setting up the store displays and dressing the mannequins.

A job as a sales associate is a great way to learn about how clothing is sold and what people like to wear. It gives you an opportunity to experience many different parts of the fashion business. Many sales associates go on to become store managers or buyers. A college degree is not required for this position, but you may need one if you want to work your way up in the company.

Be a Fashion Insider: Media

When you look at fashion magazines, do you wish you were the one writing the stories? Would you like to choose the clothes to be featured? Can you imagine spending hours sifting through new beauty products and making recommendations? Are you interested in interviewing designers and models? Do you wonder what happens behind the scenes of a photo shoot? Do you enjoy research and writing? If any of these things excite you, then you might want to consider a career in fashion media.

Fashion Editor

Fashion editors work for magazines, newspapers, websites, and television. They set the tone for what each month's issue will focus on. For example, *Teen Vogue* and *Seventeen* magazine both come out with a special prom issue every spring. A fashion editor is responsible for deciding what stories will appear in the magazine. This means hiring and assigning stories to journalists and photographers while at the same time working with the magazine's advertising department to decide where each ad will be placed in the publication. Many workdays are spent in the office, attending meetings and coming up with story ideas. The more exciting days are spent at fashion shows and meeting with new designers. This is one job where a strong knowledge of fashion, marketing, and writing is a must.

GO GLOSSI

Would you like to practice being a fashion editor right now? You can! Glossi lets you create your own online lookbooks, fashion magazines, and catalogs. The website provides how-to guides to walk you through the process of setting everything up. Why not try setting up a magazine with a few of your friends? You can practice designing pages and assigning stories. *Liv Magazine*, created by two thirteen-year-old girls, is on Glossi's website. The magazine talks about fashion, makeup, and back-to-school supplies. Check it out and see if it inspires you to come up with your own online magazine.

Fashion Journalist

If you would like to work for a print magazine or an online publication, then be prepared to juggle many roles. You need to know how to research and write stories. A strong sense of style and a passion for fashion are necessary for this job. You will be giving advice and reporting on trends that will influence thousands of people. Choosing a career in fashion journalism will most likely require a college degree in journalism or creative writing. To increase your chances of writing for the fashion industry, an internship at a fashion magazine will help. Another route is to take some classes or earn a certification from a fashion school along with your journalism degree. Either way, it's a competitive industry, so every bit of experience will help.

You can start working toward your future career right now. Create a blog, website, or YouTube channel. Use them to fine-tune your writing skills by posting articles or scripted videos about fashion-related events or news. Practice different types of writing styles like interviews, product reviews, and fashion runway reporting. You may find that you prefer one style over another. Ask your parents to help you find websites to publish your articles. The internet is a great place to experiment and to see how other people respond to you.

Most print magazines now have a website as well. The websites have the advantage of being able to post instant updates, whereas print magazines must wait until the next scheduled issue. Even though some of the information on a company's website is a repeat of what's in the print magazine, they both still need to have some unique articles. That's the only way to keep readers happy. And print won't completely disappear, even with technology—many people still like to flip through the glossy pages of a print magazine when they are looking at clothing.

CAREERS FOR FASHION JOURNALISTS

Fashion magazines: With over two hundred different fashion magazines in print every month,[17] the industry needs a lot of writers. Some of these writers work for the magazine full-time, and others are freelance writers. Usually a magazine's website will have information for writers who are interested in sending in their writing for publication. Look for the website section called Submission Guidelines and see how you can be featured in the magazine.

Trade publications: Keep people in the fashion industry up-to-date on the latest fashion news. If you write for a fashion trade publication, then you do a lot of reporting. You cover everything from runway shows and industry events to people working in the industry. Some of the most popular trade publications include *Women's Wear Daily*, *Footwear News*, *Accessories Magazine*, and *Textile World*.

Fashion websites: People can now log on to the internet and receive information about the runway shows at a fashion week in real time. They can receive fashion advice for any occasion and click a button to purchase the items they read about. People who write for websites have to be savvy when it comes to using social media, videos, and photographs. These are all skills you can learn right now by doing some experimenting on your computer. You can usually get your own free website from your internet service provider or from whomever supplies your email account.

Fashion blogs: They can be very similar to a person's diary, where the writer shares personal feelings about different clothing or what's happening in the industry. Most of these blogs are written by only one person, so that writer has to be responsible enough to post stories often to keep readers interested.

Names: Luisa Cameron and Fernanda Cameron
Ages: 14 and 12
Job: Magazine and blog founders

SISTERS LUISA (AGE FOURTEEN) AND FERNANDA (AGE TWELVE) HAVE A VERY COOL HOBBY. THEY LIKE TO CREATE MAGAZINES AND SUPPORT CHARITIES. IN 2010, AT THE AGES OF TWELVE AND TEN, THE SISTERS CREATED THE ONLINE MAGAZINE *SISMAGAZINE*. THE MAGAZINE, AND NOW THE RELATED BLOG, *SIS/BLOG*, INCLUDE FASHION PHOTOGRAPHY, INTERVIEWS, SKETCHES, AND REVIEWS. THE SISTERS CONTACTED LOCAL BUSINESSES AND SOON AVERAGED THIRTY ADVERTISEMENTS PER ISSUE. IN 2011 THEY BEGAN DONATING 10 PERCENT OF THEIR PROFITS TO DIRECT RELIEF, WHICH DELIVERS MEDICINES AND SUPPLIES TO PEOPLE ACROSS THE WORLD. THEY'VE BEEN FEATURED IN *TEEN VOGUE* AND ENJOY EXPLORING THEIR CREATIVITY THROUGH FASHION AND THE ARTS.

How did you come up with the idea for your magazine?
As little girls, we were always making things together. We were the type of sisters who painted together on rainy days and created imaginary worlds in our garden. The idea for *SiS* came to us in the summer of 2010. We were just two kids who didn't know what to do with their lazy summer afternoons. We were lying out in the sun reading magazines when the idea came to us: let's make our own magazine! We were so excited about our new project. In fact, that very day the idea was conceived we had our first photo shoot.

TEEN VOGUE TREND BOOKS

Each fashion season after the fashion runway shows end, *Teen Vogue* creates trend books that become the magazine's inspiration for the next six months. The editors cut out pictures of runway looks they like. These cutouts look like paper dolls. From the paper dolls, the editors notice themes they can develop into trends. For example, if a lot of designers used plaid fabric in their collections, *Teen Vogue* might develop a theme called Pretty in Plaid. The *Vogue* editors create forty folders for forty trends and put approximately thirty paper dolls in each folder. Each folder can be developed into a mood board. The editors decide which trend will be included in which magazine issue for the next six months. Then each trend folder is assigned to a stylist to develop into a larger story. Six months later, when the next runway show rolls around, they start the process all over again!

How do you use fashion to express yourselves?
We don't use fashion to express ourselves as much as we do every creative medium. For us, expression comes out of painting, drawing, taking pictures, and making films.

Who has inspired you?
So many people have inspired us but mainly our circle of

friends. We know so many creative, talented teens and adults who have been inspiring us since SiS started!

How do you balance school and work responsibilities?
It's hard to balance *SiS* on top of school, homework, sports, and extracurriculars. Since we are constantly busy, it's difficult for us to make time for being creative. We try to do the majority of our work with *SiS* on the weekends and also during holidays.

What do you like the most about your job?
The best thing about our job is working together doing something we love.

What is the most challenging thing about your job?
The most challenging aspect of *SiS* is juggling everything on top of school. We have great ideas all the time, but we have to wait until we are free to develop those ideas.

What have you done to grow your website traffic?
Website traffic and followers aren't a big concern for us. *SiS* is an outlet, a way for us to escape. It is a collection of images from our lives, a visual archive of our creative endeavors. We don't care how many likes we get or how many people have seen our blog, but we do like getting positive feedback from our family and friends. It makes us want to create more!

How has being involved with Direct Relief changed you?
Donating our proceeds to Direct Relief opened our eyes. Before we knew anything about websites and blogs, we thought being charitable wasn't possible through blogging. But after selling advertisements, we made a little money and decided to give to Direct Relief.

Where do you see yourself in ten years?
In ten years, Luisa would like to be a creative director. Fernanda aspires to work in fashion, film, and marine biology.

What advice would you give to other kids who want to start a blog?

Stay inspired. Stay motivated. Don't be afraid to take a camera everywhere you go. Document your life! Take lots of pictures and write every day.

Grace Coddington: The Michelangelo of Fashion

If you look at the front row of any major fashion show, you will see Grace Coddington. Born in Anglesey, Wales, in 1941, she has seen many changes in the fashion industry. She began reading *Vogue* in her teens and began modeling at age seventeen. In the 1960s she became a fashion editor for British *Vogue*, and in 1988 she moved to the United States to become *Vogue's* fashion director. By 1995 she was *Vogue's* creative director. She has worked with some of the best models and celebrities in the industry, styling some of the magazine's most famous photo shoots.

In 2007 cameras followed Anna Wintour, *Vogue's* editor, as her staff put together the magazine's largest issue ever in the documentary *The September Issue*. Most people who watched the movie were already familiar with Wintour as she was generally thought to be the inspiration for the magazine editor played by Meryl Streep in the movie *The Devil Wears Prada*. What viewers did not expect was the no-nonsense

Coddington and her witty sense of humor. She puts together photo spreads in *Vogue* that are more than just pictures. They tell a story. As *Time* magazine stated in 2009: "If Wintour is the Pope . . . , Coddington is Michelangelo, trying to paint a fresh version of the Sistine Chapel twelve times a year."[18] Whether it's re-creating *The Wizard of Oz* with modern-day fashion or making Mike Tyson relatable, Coddington is a genius at creating memorable photo spreads.

Her book, *Grace: A Memoir*, released in 2012, is a great read for anyone interested in a history lesson in fashion. She has worked with almost every famous designer, photographer, and model and has a story to tell for each one of them. The way she generates new ideas and styles them into a photo shoot is magical and educational. If you are looking for inspiration, then this may be the book for you!

For so many years, fashion was shrouded in mystery, this glamorous profession that people knew very little about; they thought it was so glamorous. It now has become so available, with the internet, with shops like H&M and Target that do designer collaborations, so it's more available to everyone and that's created more interest.

NINA GARCIA*

Fashion Blogger

Fashion blogs have become one of the most popular places for people to find fashion information and advice. Some of these bloggers focus on fashion they see people wearing on the street or outfits they put together out of their own closets. Others report on fashion designers and trends. The most successful blogs all have one thing in common: they all reflect the personality of their writer. If you're going to create a blog, write about things you are passionate about! Your readers will appreciate your enthusiasm.

A blog lets you show your creativity because each one is unique. You decide everything from how the page is set up to what stories you write and even how often you update the blog with new material. Go online and take a look at how different fashion bloggers have expressed themselves. A few blogs you might want to take note of are:

- ✄ *Refinery29*, which covers every aspect of fashion including runway shows, interviews with designers, and style tips and receives over thirty million visitors every year

- ✄ *Who's that Girl?* written by a thirteen-year-old girl in London who blogs about random things that she likes

- ✄ *Sincerely, Jules*, written by a cool California girl who writes each post like she is talking to her best friend

Each of these blogs is different from the others, but all of them share a love for fashion. What are some of your favorite fashion blogs?

Name: Lauren Sherman
Job: Editor at large

LAUREN SHERMAN IS THE EDITOR AT LARGE FOR *FASHIONISTA*, WHICH IS THE WORLD'S TOP SITE FOR FASHION NEWS. SHE WAS A REPORTER FOR *FORBES* MAGAZINE FROM 2006 TO 2010. IN 2009 SHE LAUNCHED HER OWN WEBSITE CALLED *THE FASHION BEAT*, BEFORE LANDING A DIGITAL EDITING JOB FROM *LUCKY* MAGAZINE.

When did you discover your love for fashion and blogging?

I was a reporter at a business publication, mostly writing about the fashion industry. When I left that job at the end of 2009, I started a blog called *The Fashion Beat*, where I wrote about the intersection between the consumer side of fashion and the business side. The people who run *Fashionista* took note of it and asked me to join the site and do the same thing for them.

What do you like most about your job?

I enjoy telling stories and making niche topics interesting to a broader audience.

What is the most challenging thing about your job?

Since going freelance at the beginning of 2013, I've been writing for a lot of publications. Sometimes it's hard to balance everything. I've had to learn to say no to assignments, which is difficult.

Where do your story ideas come from?
Mostly from observing. Sometimes another reporter will write something and one little nugget will be an idea to me. Or I'll notice something interesting at a fashion week. I also just ask people all the time what I should write about. Everyone has an opinion and sometimes those opinions are great.

Describe your typical day.
I get up, eat breakfast, write, report, do more reporting, do more writing. I'm answering emails constantly. I usually go out at night to various events. Sometimes my day will include lots of events and meetings, which means I take my laptop with me.

So many people have become bloggers now—how can new writers make themselves stand out?
There are very few writers who voice their opinion. If you've got a strong point of view, people will listen.

Where do you see yourself in ten years?
Hopefully still doing this! I'd like to write a book or two as well.

What advice would you give kids aspiring to become bloggers?
Write every day. The more you write, the better you get. It can be learned.

Bryanboy: Twitterpated about Fashion

How would you feel if famous fashion designer Marc Jacobs named a handbag after you? Bryan Yambao, better known as Bryanboy, knows exactly how that feels because it happened to him in 2008. Blogs in 2004 weren't common like they are today, but that didn't stop him from creating one. Never at a loss for words, his honesty and humor won him many fans. Today, he has over 500,000 Twitter followers, and 1.4 million unique website visits each month.[19] He is credited as being one of the first to virtually empty his shopping bags and comment on his newest clothing buys. Now when he comments on a piece of clothing he likes, it sells out immediately. A regular at fashion week, he is often seen sitting in the front row. He is photographed almost as much as the models. In 2012, his knowledge of fashion and celebrity status earned him a place on *America's Next Top Model* as a judge. What started out as a travel journal has come a very long way for Bryanboy.

Activity

Create Your Own Blog

1. Start by researching other fashion blogs. Are you interested in creating a general fashion blog, or would you like to be more specific? Do you

want this blog to be about you and your style and inspirations? Or are you happier reporting trends and other people's style? After you've made that decision, it's time to set up your blog.

2. Choose an online tool to help you set up your blog. Blogger, Tumblr, and WordPress are some of the most popular free tools. Decide which one is most suited for what you want to do.

3. After you've picked your tool, follow the online instructions on how to set up your new blog.

EXTREME BLOG MAKEOVER

✄ Keep the look of your blog simple. Don't clutter it up with a ton of stuff. Keep the focus on your blog posts.

✄ Include an About the Author section where you can tell your readers who you are. Make sure to have your parents' approval before posting anything about yourself.

✄ Add pictures to your posts. This is a fashion blog, so you must show fashion!

✄ Talk to your readers when you write your post. Invite them to make comments. Readers will visit your site more if they feel like they are involved with it.

✄ Have a Comments section after each of your blog posts. This way your readers can interact with each other—and you.

4. Building an audience takes time, so decide how often you want to update your blog. It's best to post something once or twice a day.

5. Start writing. A post doesn't have to be long to be good. You can put up photographs, stories, and videos. If you like it, chances are that other people will like it too.

6. Promote yourself. You have to let other people know about your blog to get readers. A great way to do this is to comment on other fashion blogs. You can also set up an account on any of the social media sites to talk about your blog.

7. Be patient. It will take time for readers to find you. Keep writing and promoting your blog, and readers will find you.

PROS AND CONS OF BEING A FASHION BLOGGER

Fashion bloggers usually work for themselves. Many times, you work out of your home office. The job may include going to retail stores to see new clothes and accessories, taking photographs, conducting interviews, or reviewing products. Making a true connection with your audience is the most important aspect to being a fashion blogger. You want to make sure people keep coming back to your site to read what you have to say.

Pros

✄ You can choose your own hours and work from home.

✄ Start-up costs are low. You only need a computer and a camera.

✄ You have a creative outlet to express yourself and your interests.

✄ Brands may send you free products to review for your website.

✄ Writing can lead to a career in brand blogging, social media, or fashion publicity.

✄ Some fashion bloggers go on to write books or collaborate with designers on projects.

✄ A blog looks great on a résumé or college application.

✄ Blogging lets you reach people all over the world.

Cons

✄ The learning curve for creating a blog and making it look good may be steep.

✄ You may face criticism for expressing your opinions, so be prepared to have a thick skin.

✄ It can take a long time to gain readers.

✄ You have a lot of competition, so you must always be searching for ways to stand out.

✄ You will spend a lot of time promoting your blog on other social media sites.

Cons (continued)

✂   It's difficult to make money writing a blog, so you may need a second job.

✂   You will spend many hours on your blog, so you must love what you are doing!

9

Lights, Camera, Fashion: Model and Photographer

When the camera flashes go off, would you rather be the person behind the camera or the one in front? Fashion photographers and models are keys to a designer's success. They give regular people an opportunity to see a designer's new clothes through photographs. This is usually the first impression the general public has of the clothes. The right photo and model can sell a ton of clothes!

Fashion Model

Fashion models appear in everything from magazines and catalogs to advertising campaigns and walk in runway shows. They fly all over the world to shoot in exciting locations and to appear in designers' shows. However, the job isn't all travel and glamour. A lot of time is spent on researching casting calls, attending agency meetings, and maintaining how you look.

The first thing you want to do is put together a portfolio. This is a fashion model's résumé in photographs. It is your most important tool to promote yourself. You should include pictures that show your range as a model. Look at your photos and ask yourself: Am I showing different facial expressions and body poses? Do I know how to tell a story with the way I interact with the camera? This is what people will be looking at when they view your portfolio.

MODELING SCHOOLS

Many people who are interested in modeling are tempted to sign up for modeling school classes. These schools are usually seen as a waste of money by people who work in the modeling industry. They can sometimes cost a lot of money, and they are not in a position to offer modeling jobs. If a modeling agency is interested in you, then the professionals there will take the time to teach you how to do a runway walk and pose for photographs.

On the other hand, modeling schools can have some benefits if you are realistic about what you will get out of the classes. They do offer practice walking and makeup tips. A lot of time is focused on manners, poise, and etiquette. This is what charm schools used to offer. Having these additional skills may give you some extra self-confidence when you want to present yourself for a job. It's also a great way to meet other teens who are interested in modeling. Department stores often offer modeling classes that last a full day and are more affordable.

Most models work for an agency. Do your research and make sure the agencies you are looking at have a good reputation. One way to find the names of modeling agencies is to look in your favorite magazines to see who represents your favorite models. Look up any agencies you have questions about on the internet. Don't go to any appointments until you've done your homework. Not every modeling agency is the same. Some act more as modeling schools and aren't known for finding modeling assignments.

As a model, you go on a lot of casting calls, or go-sees. These are auditions for modeling jobs. Show up to these interviews confident and on time. Wear something simple and keep your makeup light. The people hiring want to see your face and body without distractions. Be enthusiastic and let them see the real you. Let them know how much you want the job. Before you leave, give the casting director your comp card. A comp card includes three to five of your best pictures along with your name, contact information, and physical measurements. This is a great way for them to remember you and to see how you photograph.

Scott Schuman: The Satorialist

Some people find success just by doing something they love, by following their passion. This is what happened to Scott Schuman, who founded the blog *The Satorialist* in 2005. His blog visually documents fashion through everyday street style and designer runway shows.

In 2005 Schuman quit his job to be a stay-at-home dad to his two girls. With a camera in hand, he hit the streets to photograph real people who had great style. He posted these pictures on his blog, and people in the fashion industry began to take notice.

He has participated in advertising campaigns for the Gap, Verizon, and Kiehl's skincare products. He shot the social media sensation "Art of the Trench" series for Burberry. His work has appeared in *Vogue Italia*, *Vogue Paris*, and *Interview* magazine. GQ magazine reserved a page for him in every issue for three years running. In 2009 he published a book with his favorite images.

A Day in the Life of a Fashion Model During New York Fashion Week

6:30 AM   Wake up, eat breakfast, and shower.

7:30 AM   Call agent to make sure none of the information about the fashion shows have changed.

8:00 AM   Arrive at the first show. Get hair and makeup done.

10:45 AM   Get into the first runway outfit.

11:00 AM   Start first runway show.

11:45 AM   Hurry to the second show and get hair and makeup done and clothing on just in time for show to start.

1:00 PM   Finish the second show and catch a cab over to a Ralph Lauren fitting for an upcoming show.

1:45 PM   Leave Ralph Lauren and grab lunch on the way to a casting call.

4:00 PM   Arrive at a third runway show to get hair and makeup done.

| 7:00 PM | Line up for the runway show. |
| 9:00 PM | Find dinner. |

*My job as a portrait photographer is
to seduce, amuse, and entertain.*

HELMUT NEWTON*

Name: Hayley Wheeler
Age: 18
Job: Fashion model

EIGHTEEN-YEAR-OLD HAYLEY WHEELER WAS DISCOVERED IN A PARKING LOT BY A MODEL SCOUT WHEN SHE WAS THIRTEEN YEARS OLD. IN 2011, AT THE AGE OF SIXTEEN, SHE MOVED FROM HER HOMETOWN OF CHARDON, OHIO, TO NEW YORK CITY AS PART OF A *PRIMETIME NIGHTLINE* NEWS SPECIAL IN WHICH FOUR TEENS MOVED TO THE BIG CITY TO START THEIR MODELING CAREERS. SINCE THEN, SHE HAS BEEN FEATURED IN MANY DESIGNER ADVERTISING CAMPAIGNS AND HAS TRAVELED THE WORLD DOING PHOTO SHOOTS. SHE IS REPRESENTED BY NEXT MODEL MANAGEMENT, WORLDWIDE; SIGHT MODEL MANAGEMENT, SPAIN; CHIC MANAGEMENT, AUSTRALIA; AND MOTHER MODEL MANAGEMENT. SHE HAS COME A LONG WAY SINCE LEAVING OHIO.

What are some of your projects?

I have done editorials, commercial shoots, runway shows, campaigns, and presentations. To name a few, I have worked with *Seventeen*, *FLATT*, *HUF*, *Industry*, and *Palm Springs Life* magazine. I have done commercial shoots for Oscar de la Renta, G by Guess, Juicy Couture, Delia's, Sporty Girl, Cotton On, Jason Wu, The One, Duffie Jeans, Equipment, Amazon, Avon, Lord & Taylor, Theory, Keepsake the Label, Blood Orange, Group USA, Hyundai, Bloomingdale's, Macy's, Saks Fifth Avenue, Necessary Clothing, Express, etc. I recently did the David Jones, Myer, and Kardashian runway shows. A fun shoot was a G by Guess campaign for *Fast & Furious 6*. It was shot in Los Angeles with fast cars from the movie. Lots of fun!

When did you discover your love for modeling?

I was approached many times by scouts, and one day asked my parents if I could model to pay for my own college. I fell in love with it and wanted to make a career of it.

How did you get started?

I started off locally through Cleveland, Chicago, and the Carolina markets. I met Jeff and Mary Clarke, of Mother Model Management, and then signed with Next Model Management, New York, and Next Model Management, Worldwide. I'm currently with Next Model Management, Worldwide; Chic Model Management, Australia; and Sight Model Management, Spain.

What do you like most about modeling?

I enjoy traveling; experiencing different cultures, foods, landscapes; and meeting new people.

What is the most challenging part of the job?

I would have to say that not being able to spend a lot of time with family and friends is the most challenging. My home is where my work is, and I never know from one day to the next where I am going and how long I will stay. It is also challenging to make plans or commitments as everything changes daily.

What has been one of the most exciting moments you've had since you got started?
There is one thing that, unfortunately, I cannot say at the moment but was my highlight and hopefully will happen for me. Recently, I got to spend three months in Australia, which is a place I always wanted to visit—a true paradise for me.

Where do you see yourself in ten years?
I see myself working hard in the fashion industry and continuing to grow within the industry. I love it!

What advice would you give kids aspiring to be models?
I would say: chase your dreams, follow your heart, and never give up.

Activity
Model like a pro

✄ Practice posing in front of a mirror.

✄ Make your limbs look long and lean by keeping them from blending with your body or each other: lift your arms slightly away from your sides and slightly spread your legs.

✄ Make you neck look longer by rolling your shoulders back and pushing your face forward.

- Keep your hand loose like a ballerina, graceful and soft.

- Pretend a wire is pulling your spine up to the ceiling. No slouching!

- Show off your curves by angling your body so your backside is slightly facing the camera. Toss your hair over your shoulder and give a look back.

- Put your hands on your hips to create a smaller waist.

- Practice movement poses, like running and jumping.

- Use your clothing or accessories as props. A flowing dress gives you a lot of opportunities to show movement.

- Create a natural smile by thinking of something really funny.

- Pose like a celebrity by putting one hand on your hip and slightly bend one knee.

- Change your pose every three seconds to keep things interesting.

- Don't always look directly into the camera.

✂ Look at fashion magazines to gather inspiration and new ideas.

✂ Have fun with the camera, and don't be afraid to try new things!

There's a button that goes On, and I'm On. And when I go On, there is almost no me; there is just a character who is doing all this.

GISELE BUNDCHEN*

TOOLS OF THE TRADE

Just like handymen wouldn't show up to work without their toolboxes, models should never show up to a photo shoot without their toolkits. Not every modeling job will include a makeup artist, hairstylist, and clothing stylist. Many times you have to be prepared to do any or all of these jobs. If you show up to a photo shoot with freshly washed hair, well groomed, and organized for the job, it shows that you are a professional. A photographer and client will always remember the models who show up ready to work. A well-packed modeling toolkit makes it easier to deal with any situation—and makes a great first impression! Here's some of the items you may want to consider packing:

- Clear deodorant
- Face wipes
- Hair clips and bands
- Hairspray
- High-heeled shoes
- Lint brush
- Makeup
- Moisturizer
- Nude and black undergarments
- Portable mirror
- Safety pins and clips
- Water and snacks

In a portrait, you have room to have a point of view. The image may not be literally what's going on, but it's representative.

Annie Leibovitz*

Fashion Photographer

Can you picture yourself jetting off from one exotic location to another taking pictures? Or designers begging you to take photographs of their runway shows? This may be what you picture when you think of fashion photographers, but few people get these kinds of opportunities. With hard work, you can become a successful photographer. There's a lot of demand for people who can take pictures for catalogs, magazines, advertising, and online publications. With a little planning you can become one of those people.

A great way to begin is to start studying photography. Look at pictures in books and fashion magazines. What kinds of stories do the pictures tell? Look at pictures that are artistic, along with photos that are trying to sell a product. What makes them different? What makes them the same? If you start to study some of the more famous photographers, you will start to notice that you can recognize their work. Photographers are like artists, and they each have a different style.

If you want to take pictures for a living, then you need to know how to use a camera. Try out different types of cameras and lenses to see what you like. A school or community photography class will introduce you to a lot of different equipment. Photographers transfer their photos to a computer so they can use software to retouch or make a photo look better. Some of the most popular software is Capture One Pro, Adobe Photoshop, and Adobe Lightroom. Many computers now come preloaded with some sort of photo editing software. Try editing some of your own photographs to see how much you can change a picture.

A photographer needs to take a lot of . . . photographs! Nothing beats practice. Try taking portraits, which are pictures taken from the shoulders up. Take full-length pictures and notice how different poses affect the quality of the images. See if you can tell a story with your pictures. This can be done with facial expressions, poses, costumes, and the settings you choose. It's important to let your personality show in your photographs.

Once you have a lot of good pictures to choose from, it's time to make a portfolio. A portfolio is a book of your work. You will show this book to prospective colleges, employers, and clients. This is where you put your best pictures, the photos that best represent your style. You can create an online gallery too, which may give your work a bigger audience. An online gallery shows people that you know how to use technology and can apply it to your work.

Another very important aspect of this job is for you to know fashion. You need to know what the current styles and trends are because you need to understand how you should style your photo shoot. If you are going to work with a designer, then you must know about that person's clothes and what type of customer the clothes are for. For example, Ralph Lauren is known for his all-American style of clothes. His photo campaigns often show young people in casual settings wearing his preppy clothes. Betsey Johnson is known for her fun and feminine dresses. Her advertising campaigns are bright and almost cartoonish. As a photographer, you need to know how to work with designers who have very different needs.

One way to gain experience is by taking a photography class at school and entering local photo contests. You can also create a website to showcase your work and speak to other kids who are interested in photography. In college it is common to apply for a photography internship or a job as a photo assistant. This gives you a firsthand look at the industry. You will learn how to work with clients, stylists, models, and art directors. Anything you can do to increase your knowledge and contacts in the photography industry will help you to get the job you want.

IN VOGUE *profile*

Name: Susan Jeffers
Job: Photographer

WHEN SUSAN JEFFERS WAS FOURTEEN YEARS OLD, A PALM READER LOOKED AT HER PALM AND SAID SHE SAW HER "EYES IN A BOX." TEN YEARS LATER, JEFFERS BECAME A PROFESSIONAL PHOTOGRAPHER. HER WORK HAS APPEARED IN *HARPER'S BAZAAR*, *REDBOOK*, AND *INTERVIEW* MAGAZINE. SHE LIVES IN FLORIDA,

How did you obtain the skills to become a fashion photographer?

I was initially teaching myself, and then I enrolled at the University of South Florida to receive my bachelor's degree in fine arts. I submitted a portfolio and was entered in at the highest level.

What are some of the projects you've worked on?

My favorite thing to do is to collaborate with my team. Right now we are working on a project together for the holidays called Good Will to All Men. This fashion spread shows people how to shop on a budget with clothes featured from, yes, Goodwill. Our projects have included artists like the Orlando Ballet dancers, who have appeared in local fashion magazines with us, to regular, everyday people who need their campaigns documented on websites, billboards, or business cards.

What is the most challenging aspect of your job?

Carrying my heavy gear and sitting in front of a computer for hours on end editing, but I love it all. Be prepared for some back and neck pain.

Where do you get your inspiration for photo shoots?

I oftentimes have these eureka moments in my sleep. Of course they are inspired from things I read or see, but with my own twist . . . the team's twist.

How much collaboration is involved when you are doing a photo shoot for a client?

One has to know their client. Some clients like to take a backseat, and some need full control. You know right away because your clients are usually very up front with you. One should never overstep boundaries.

What advice would you give to kids aspiring to be photographers?

Try not to compare yourself with too many other photographers. In fact, really try and not even look at their work too much in the beginning. To acquire your own unique signature, you need to draw from your feelings and daily experiences. Remember that the person you are capturing has their own soul. Do what is right for them and capture their essence. In doing so, people will see your soul in it.

FASHION PHOTOGRAPHERS YOU SHOULD KNOW

Mario Testino: Born in Peru, this fashion photographer has photographed both Princess Diana and Kate Middleton. He has taken pictures for some of the most famous advertising campaigns for designers Gucci, Versace, and Chanel.

Steven Meisel: This New York fashion photographer has helped launch the careers of many supermodels by making his subjects look elegant and creatively telling stories with his photos. His photographs of Madonna for one of her album covers put him in the public eye and increased his popularity. He has shot the pictures for every monthly *Vogue Italia* cover for the last twenty years.

Annie Leibovitz: Born in Connecticut, Leibovitz spent the first thirteen years of her career taking pictures for *Rolling Stone* magazine before moving to *Vanity Fair* magazine. She is known for her bold use of colors and the unusual way she poses her subjects. She has photographed models, musicians, celebrities, and politicians.

Steven Klein: Originally from Rhode Island, he brings the fine arts to his photography. He is known for his *W* editorials. He is talented at making celebrities look different than people are used to seeing them. His photographs of Justin Timberlake, Britney Spears, and Brad Pitt are a great example of this.

Albert Watson: This Scottish photographer has created over 250 *Vogue* cover shoots. He's created advertisements for Gap, Levi's, and Chanel. He also directs commercials and writes books.

Bill Cunningham: Born in Massachusetts, he is known as the original street fashion photographer. Working for the *New York Times*, he rides a bicycle around Manhattan, taking pictures of everyday people on the street. He is interested in how people use fashion in their day-to-day lives. In 2010 a documentary called *Bill Cunningham New York* was released about his working life.

FASHION AND PHOTOGRAPHY BOOKS

Are you looking for a little inspiration? Models and photographers are always looking for new ways to express themselves. Go to your local bookstore or library and check out the following books. They will give you a whole new perspective on modeling, photography, and fashion.

- ✄ *Carine Roitfeld: Irreverent*, photography by Carine Roitfeld

- ✄ *Dior Couture*, photography by Patrick Demarchelier

- ✄ *W: The First 40 Years*, edited by Stefano Tonchi with Christopher Bagley

- ✄ *Terrywood*, photography by Terry Richardson

- ✄ *Tom Ford* by Bridget Foley and Tom Ford

- ✄ *Vogue: The Editor's Eye* by Conde Naste

- ✄ *Decades: A Century of Fashion* by Cameron Silver

- ✄ *Harper's Bazaar: Greatest Hits* by Glenda Bailey

- ✄ *Marc Jacobs* by Bridget Foley

- ✄ *Tim Walker: Story Teller*, photography by Tim Walker

Quiz

Which Side of the Camera Should You Be On?

You know you like fashion, and you know you like photographs, so are you better suited to be a photographer or a model? Some people like to see pictures of themselves, and others would prefer to catch fashion on film. Take this quiz to see if you should be posing for pictures or taking them.

1. At a party I am . . .
   a. In every picture
   b. Running around with my camera, trying to capture the moment
   c. Not aware of cameras or photographs being taken

2. When I appear in photographs, I am . . .
   a. Perfectly posed and showing my best side
   b. Sticking out my tongue or acting crazy
   c. Photos? What photos?

3. When I go shopping, I . . .
   a. Take selfies of every outfit I try on
   b. Am a people watcher
   c. Hang out with friends and have a great time

4. When it comes to my body, I am . . .
   a. Disciplined about eating healthy and exercising
   b. Not concerned about how it looks on film
   c. Involved in physical activities for fun

5. When it comes to my skin care routine, I . . .
   a. Follow a skin routine every morning and night
   b. Take care of any skin issues that come up
   c. Don't have a routine

6. When I look in the mirror, I . . .
   a. Like to practice different poses and facial
      expressions
   b. Am doing something like brushing my teeth,
      putting on my makeup, or combing my hair
   c. Make funny faces

7. When it comes to walking in heels, I . . .
   a. Can strut my stuff with no problem
   b. Would rather never wear them
   c. Would only practice walking in them if I knew I
      had to wear them for an upcoming event

If you answered mostly A's, then you might enjoy being in
front of the camera as a model. Start practicing your walk
and runway poses. It can be a fun job that takes you all

over the world. Modeling is harder than it looks, so you'll need to do your homework.

If you answered mostly B's, you're more comfortable behind the camera. Photography is a great career with a lot of opportunities. Practice taking photos and don't be afraid to experiment. Consider taking random pictures of people at the mall. Inspiration is everywhere.

If you answered mostly C's, then you might not be interested in being a model or a photographer. That's okay! There are so many other great career options in fashion for you to explore.

10

Fashion as a Career

Now you've officially decided you want a career in fashion. You may be asking yourself, what do I do now? It may seem overwhelming to start planning your career right now, while you are busy with school, friends, and activities. It doesn't have to be. So many things you do every day help you to prepare for your future. When you are getting dressed in the morning, you are interacting with fashion as you choose what clothes to wear. When you turn in a well-written paper at school, you are developing skills you can use as a fashion journalist or after your modeling career is over. Fashion is everywhere, so have fun with it!

Doing collections, doing fashion
is like a nonstop dialogue.

KARL LAGERFELD*

If you want to work in fashion and make money doing it, be prepared to run into some skeptics. Some people consider a fashion career a difficult way to earn a living. Some objections you may hear are:

- ✂ If you go to a fashion school and the career doesn't work out, then you won't have a bachelor's degree to fall back on.

- ✂ What are the chances that you will be the next Ralph Lauren or Coco Chanel?

- ✂ You'll have to live in New York, and it's too expensive to live there.

- ✂ Blogging is a hobby and not a career.

- ✂ You don't even know how to sew.

One way to make people feel better about your decision to work in fashion is to do your homework. Research the fashion industry. Read everything you can about fashion career opportunities. Question everything you don't understand. Choosing a career is a huge decision! If people see you taking it seriously, then they are more likely to take it seriously too.

SEVEN WAYS TO LEARN MORE ABOUT FASHION CAREERS

- ✂ Find a mentor. Anytime you are around someone who works in fashion, ask that person questions. If you take a job or internship in retail, you will have plenty of opportunities to learn from other people.

- ✄ Write fashion articles for your school newspaper or find websites where you can contribute. Many websites love receiving free content.

- ✄ Read books and watch documentaries about famous people in fashion.

- ✄ Go to fashion shows. Many cities host runway events for local talent. Also, larger department stores often host back-to-school fashion events.

- ✄ Take sewing classes. Even if you're not interested in being a designer, it's important to know how a garment is put together. For example, a blogger or public relations person will use this information to spot how well a garment is made.

- ✄ Take pictures of people you see on the street. Look at the photos and see what you like and don't like about their clothes. The more you expose yourself to fashion, the better you will understand what you like.

- ✄ Watch the New York Fashion Week runway shows on the internet.

IN VOGUE *profile*

Name: Nicole Flood
Job: Fashion designer

DO YOU HAVE CLOTHES IN YOUR CLOSET THAT YOU NO LONGER WEAR? DID YOU KNOW YOU CAN TAKE THOSE CLOTHES AND TURN THEM INTO A NEW CREATION? THAT'S EXACTLY WHAT

Nicoloe Flood did when she started her design business! Her hats and clothing are made from 100 percent recycled material. She doesn't shop at fabric stores. She goes to thrift stores and makes something beautiful out of other people's discards. This makes her pieces unique. She started Flood Clothing in Portland, Oregon, in 2004, and is very active in the art community. Every person who buys one of her designs can be guaranteed a one-of-a-kind creation.

Where did you learn to design and sew?

I learned how to sew in home economics classes at school in eighth grade. I hated it. But then my grandma (she's been sewing professionally for over fifty years) showed me some sweet tricks to make sewing easier and more accessible. The designing part of this has always just been in my heart for as long as I can remember. Ultimately I went to the Art Institute of Portland and got my bachelor's degree in apparel design. This is where I learned to do all of the technical sewing, patterning, and honing in on design work.

What made you decide to use 100 percent recycled materials in your designs?

At first it was a by-product of necessity. Because fabric is so expensive—a project for school could end up costing over $100 to make. So, I started to go to the Goodwill to find fabrics and became completely hooked on the process of transforming something old into something new. Working within the confines of recycled clothing helps to give my creativity boundaries so that I can be more effective with it. Recycled fabrics not only have the sweet bonus of being sustainable and good for the earth, but they also give me the ability to make truly one-of-a-kind garments, which is one of the foundations of my company.

Where do you find your inspiration?
The first answer to that is life. We can't help but translate all that we see and experience into our artwork. I know that life happening impacts my designs more than I will ever be able to understand. After that, I have a subscription to a very popular Japanese fashion magazine called *Zipper*. It is geared toward teenagers, but I love the playfulness and the freedom of expression in Japanese fashion culture.

How did you start your business?
I started my business in the hallways of my college. I started selling to my classmates and taking custom orders from them there too. They were so popular that I made a little catalog with yarn samples and photos of all of the people who ordered hats from me. I would set up a suitcase in the hallways between classes and sell them to people at school. Two years after I graduated, I became a member of the Portland Saturday Market. From there I was able to generate enough revenue to explore growing my product line, develop into a better designer, and establish a clientele base that was solid enough for me to grow my business.

Do you sell your hats and clothing only through your boutique, or do you sell them in other retail locations?
For the most part, yes, I do most of my selling now directly from my own store and various shows that I travel to. There are several stores across the country and in Canada that now carry my clothing and hats.

What has been one of the most exciting moments you've had since starting in this industry?

Honestly, it is a moment that still continues to happen. It is meeting people from all walks of life—who are beautiful human beings, who love my work! To have someone who has great style and is a good person choose your clothing as a part of the expression? Gah! It is the best feeling in the world. It gets even better when they find you year after year to get new pieces. The feeling of not only being seen and supported as a designer but to have people who literally commit themselves to you because they believe in what you are doing. This is still the most exciting thing that I experience in this industry. It gives you faith that small businesses that create and sell with intention can survive and thrive!

What are some of the biggest challenges in this business?

The biggest challenge that you will face is competing with mass-produced goods. People in this country have become quite comfortable and reliant on being able to go to stores and purchase clothing at prices that are unrealistic. To create one-of-a-kind, sustainable fashion by hand and make a living is not cheap. You will not be able to compete with the prices of mainstream fashion. The trick is to strike a balance with how much product you can make well and finding the market or audience of people who can not only afford your work but understand and appreciate what it is you are doing.

The next big thing that can be really hard is defining who you are as a designer—as a clothing line. You really have to commit to yourself and somehow have the flexibility to be able to shift your vision if what you are building is not selling well or reaching the people it needs to.

Where do you see your business in ten years?

In ten years, what I want is to first still be deeply connected to my work. To still love what I do. After that, I would like to have a production house full of Portland's finest talent who will help me continue to produce my line so I can reach more people and places. To travel and share my work on the East Coast as well as other countries. I hope to be focused on my passion—designing my visions for my public line. To be spending the rest of my days working on really big projects that take months to complete. These projects would be for individuals who are wanting a very specialty piece or a group who has asked me to manifest garments that are a part of a visionary project. To continue expanding into the creator part of my spirit while staying in touch with the wholeness of my business.

What advice would you give kids who are aspiring designers?

Don't give up; don't ever stop. Whenever you make something—wear it! The world will let you know if you are moving in the right direction. Be passionate about what you are doing. The world is drawn to and loves passion. If you have made something you are passionate about, put it on yourself and go out into the world. When people ask you about it or pay you a compliment, tell them about your work. You never know who you will meet and who may be interested in buying your work. Being able to speak confidently to people about your creations makes a world of difference. Know who you are and what you stand for as a designer. This doesn't mean that you won't change as you become more experienced, but there are fundamental elements that will never change. Once you have an understanding of these elements, you can create and share your creations with full intention. People are drawn to things that are created with full awareness and intention. Don't be afraid to expose and share this true nature of yourself with others and your work. It is what will ultimately form the connection you have with your audience.

Activity

DIY Projects to Get You Started

Do you need to get those creative juices flowing? Do you want to do a small fashion project before committing to something bigger? Just because you aren't ready to start designing your first fashion collection or start a blog doesn't mean you can't do something fashion related. You don't need to run out and get a job or make another time-consuming commitment. There are a lot of fun projects you can complete in just a few hours.

Stencil a T-shirt: Designing your own T-shirts is fun and easy. Start by tracing the picture you want on your shirt onto a piece of contact paper. Cut the image out of the contact paper and stick it to a plain shirt. Use fabric paint to cover the areas you cut out. After the paint dries, peel off the stencil. Enjoy your new shirt!

Add studs or rhinestones to a pair of jeans: If you want to add a little pizazz to your jeans, then you might try adding some studs or rhinestones. You can pick these up at any fabric or craft store. They look great added to the pockets or cuffs of your jeans.

Bead a shirt collar: Do you have a button-down shirt that you never wear? You can change the entire look of a shirt by sewing beads or pearls onto the collar. Use the extra beads or pearls to make a matching bracelet.

Change the look of your ballet flats: It's easy to change the look of your shoes, and the change doesn't have to be permanent. You can clip broaches or bows to the toes of your shoes to make them look different. In five minutes or less, you will be staring at a whole new shoe.

Transform your jean shorts: Instead of letting the bottom of your cutoff jean shorts fray, why don't you add some lace? You can do this with a needle and thread or with a sewing machine.

Button up: A quick and easy way to change the look of your shirts is to sew new buttons on them. Most button-down shirts come with boring white buttons. Go to a fabric store or a thrift shop and find some interesting buttons to sew on in replacement.

Make an envelope laptop or iPad case: Making a no-sew case is fun and easy. Trace an outline of your device on a piece of felt. Cut out the felt and glue it to a piece of canvas fabric. Fold the edges and then wrap it around your device. Take a piece of thick ribbon and add a buckle to it. Glue the ribbon to the back of the case and then buckle it in front. Now you have your device wrapped in a pretty case. Enjoy!

Design is a constant challenge to balance comfort with luxe, the practical with the desirable.

DONNA KARAN*

Name: Lindsay Degen
Job: Fashion designer

IT'S HARD TO IMAGINE STARTING A CAREER BASED ON SOME-
THING YOU LEARNED TO DO AS A CHILD, BUT THAT'S EXACTLY
WHAT HAPPENED WHEN LINDSAY DEGEN'S GRANDMOTHER
TAUGHT HER TO KNIT WHEN DEGEN WAS JUST THREE. SHE
ATTENDED SCHOOL AT CENTRAL SAINT MARTINS COLLEGE OF
ARTS AND DESIGN AND THE RHODE ISLAND SCHOOL OF DESIGN
AND IMPROVED HER CRAFT BY STUDYING WITH A KNITMASTER.
IN 2011 SHE LAUNCHED A COLLECTION OF KNIT BRAS, UNDER-
WEAR, AND SOCKS. SHE INCREASED HER COLLECTION IN 2013 BY
OFFERING SWEATERS, DRESSES, AND SHOES. SHE HAS BEEN FEA-
TURED IN SOME BIG-NAME PUBLICATIONS LIKE *WOMEN'S WEAR
DAILY*, *TEEN VOGUE*, *NYLON*, *ELLE*, AND *LUCKY*.

When did you discover your love for fashion and designing?

Fashion always interested me from a young age, but I always
thought I would pursue art. When I realized that most young
artists do not get shows immediately, I decided to make more
wearable work because in the fashion industry, you can show
immediately. I started showing two times a year, during fall/
winter as well as spring/summer New York Fashion Week.

How did you transition from being a student to designing your own collection?

When I graduated, I had a studio and continued knitting. I
had no idea really what I was doing. Later that year, I got
cast for a T.J. Maxx commercial, and I flew to Los Angeles to
shoot it. There must have been hundreds of people working

on that campaign, so I just became friends with whoever was friendly. I ended up befriending the creative director on the shoot. We stayed friends, and he really pushed me to start DEGEN. Mark Fina and I still work together on all of my advertising stuff to this day.

Where do you find inspiration for your fashion designs?
Everywhere really. I generally start with inspiration from color. I look at paintings and go on adventures. I love being outside. I think a lot of the inspiration for my work just comes from experiencing things. I also draw a lot from the human body.

What do you like most about having your own line?
I love being able to work with my friends. I have a dedicated crew (teamDEGEN) who all love knitting and never expected to get paid to do it. We have a great time in the studio together.

What is the most challenging thing about having your own line?
The reality is you need money to keep the business going. The most challenging part, for me, is making sure we have a good cash flow. I often work more than twelve hours a day every day of the week. Squeezing in "me time" is sometimes hard, but I think where there is a will, there is a way.

What has been one of the most exciting moments you've had since starting your fashion career?
This year has definitely been the most rewarding year for DEGEN. I got a *Women's Wear Daily* cover, we did a whole section of the Victoria's Secret Fashion Show, and I won a huge fashion industry award. Seeing the Victoria's Secret Fashion

Show in person and then a month later on television with all of my friends was amazing.

What advice can you give kids who are interested in working in the fashion industry?
I think the best advice I could give is basically to create things that speak to them. I have always been praised for doing something different. I really am just doing me. That's important. Another thing is that you do not have to be a designer to be in the fashion industry. There are so many other really important roles to fill: styling, fashion writing, makeup, creative direction, video, web design, legal, etc.

YOU'VE GOT ME IN STITCHES

1937 *Clothes-Line*: This was the first show to focus on the history of fashion.

1980-2000 *Style with Elsa Klensch*: This show on CNN brought people interested in fashion to their televisions every Saturday morning. Credited with creating fashion television, Elsa Klensch interviewed famous designers, artists, and models. She reported about fashion from all over the world.

1985-2012 *Fashion Television*: A fashion show that got its start in Toronto, Canada, it eventually was so popular that it went into syndication in the United States on VH1, E!, and Style.

1986-2000 *The Clothes Show*: A BBC show with a cult following made catwalk trends wearable for everyday people.

1989-2000 *House of Style:* Cindy Crawford hosted this show for six years. It was the first series to give an inside look at the modeling industry.

1989-2009 *Fashion File:* The Canadian television series offered tips on modeling and how to dress for less. The "Style Icon" segments focused on fashionable celebrities and the inspiration behind their great styles.

2003-2013 *What Not to Wear:* This show targeted "fashion disasters" nominated by the "victim's" family and friends. Stylists went through closets and got rid of all unflattering clothing. Nominees went shopping for a full wardrobe makeover. They were shown how to dress for their body type and lifestyle.

2003-present *America's Next Top Model:* Hosted by former supermodel and talk show host Tyra Banks, this show features a panel of judges critiquing modeling hopefuls and their photo shoots. Banks offers the contestants pointers along the way and coined the popular term *smize*, which is when models smile with their eyes. Each week, one contestant is eliminated while the others move closer to a modeling contract. In 2013 the cast expanded to include male, as well as the usual female, contestant models.

2004-present *Project Runway:* Hosted by model Heidi Klum and fashion guru Tim Gunn, it was the first show to create a weekly fashion design contest. Every week contestants are presented with a fashion challenge for which they must work within a certain time frame and budget. The design is presented before a panel of judges during a runway show. One contestant is eliminated, while another is declared a winner. The last contestants, usually three, present at the final challenge, at New York Fashion Week.

2008-2013 *Rachel Zoe Project*: Cameras followed celebrity stylist Rachel Zoe as she styled clients, launched a clothing line, and juggled home life.

2009 *Running in Heels*: In this behind-the-scenes look at how fashion magazine *Marie Claire* is put together every month, three interns navigate the fashion world while juggling numerous assignments.

2009-2011 *The Fashion Show: Ultimate Collection*: Hosted by fashion designer Isaac Mizrahi and supermodel Iman, this show offers designers weekly design contests.

2010 *Kell on Earth*: Cameras followed Kelly Cutrone, founder of the People's Revolution, as she ran her fashion public relations firm with an iron fist. Viewers received an inside look at how fashion runway shows and events are put together.

2010-present *Fashion Police*: A weekly entertainment program in which a panel of celebrity hosts critique celebrity fashions and red carpet looks.

2010-present *Lives of Style*: Elisabeth Laurence hosts this West Coast newsmagazine show. It features the latest news from runway shows, designers, and beauty editors.

2011-present *All on the Line*: *Elle* magazine's creative director, Joe Zee, and a team of fashion industry professionals help struggling fashion designers resurrect their business. They offer everything from business advice to design pointers. After implementing changes to their business, designers are rewarded with a "meet and greet" with buyers from major retail stores.

2011-present *Fashion Hunters*: Based in a chain of high-end consignment stores called Second Time Around, the cameras follow four sales associates as they search the closets and attics of the New York fashion elite.

2011 *Project Accessory*: In this spin-off of the popular *Project Runway* show, contestants designed jewelry, handbags, and shoes.

2012-2013 *Fashion Star*: Contestants competed for a chance to have their designs bought by retail stores.

2012-2013 *It's a Brad, Brad World*: Brad Goreski, a spunky fashion stylist, gave an inside look on starting a celebrity styling business.

2013-present *The Face*: Fashion Photographer Nigel Barker hosts this modeling competition series. Super-model coaches help modeling newbies compete to become "the face" for the beauty retailer Ulta.

2014 *Under the Gunn*: Tim Gunn adds to his *Project Runway* responsibilities by hosting his own show, which pits teams of clothing designers, led by *Project Runway* alumni, against each other in design challenges.

I don't design clothes.
I design dreams.

RALPH LAUREN*

Moziah Bridges: Debonair in Bows

Who knew that a few scraps of fabric from his grand-mother's sewing box could turn into a budding business? Moziah Bridges started sewing his bow ties at age nine, and now four years later, Mo's Bows have been featured in *O, The Oprah Magazine*; *Vogue*; and *GQ*. His business motto is "Designing a colorful bow tie is just part of my vision to make the world a fun and happier place."[20] Mo isn't just satisfied with selling bow ties. He also believes in giving back to his community. Once a year, he creates a special tie where 100 percent of the proceeds goes toward sending kids to camp in his hometown of Memphis, Tennessee.

So, you absolutely know you want to work in the fashion business? Congratulations! You've made an important decision. Now it's time to narrow it down a bit. Flip back through this book, revisiting chapters, profiles, and activities that stick in your mind. Think further about those particular careers. From picking out what you're going to wear to school to holding down a seasonal job at your favorite clothing store, you are already working in fashion. Try a lot of new things. Fashion is all about expressing yourself, so have fun with it.

11

Resources

Camp Resources

Blueprint Fashion Design, bpsummerprograms.com

Camp Fashion Design, campfashiondesign.com

Fashion Camp NYC, fahioncampnyc.com

Fashion Design Camp, fashiondesigncamp.com

Modeling Camp, modelingcamp.com

Pali Adventures Fashion Camp, paliadventures.com/specialties
/fashion-institute/

University of Georgia Fashion Design Camp, georgiacenter
.uga.edu/ppd/courses/summer-academy-camps
/fashion-design-camp-ages-13-17

College Resources

West Coast
Academy of Art University, academyart.edu

California College of the Arts (CCA), cca.edu

Fashion Institute of Design and Merchandising (FIDM),
    fidm.edu

Midwest
Kent State University (KSU), www.kent.edu/artscollege/fashion/

School of the Art Institute of Chicago (SAIC), saic.edu

University of Cincinnati, uc.edu

East Coast
Drexel University, drexel.edu

Fashion Institute of Technology (FIT), fitnyc.edu

Massachusetts College of Art and Design, massart.edu

Parsons The New School for Design, newschool.edu/parsons/

Pratt Institute, pratt.edu

Rhode Island School of Design (RISD), risd.edu

Savannah College of Art and Design, scad.edu

Syracuse University, syr.edu

Resources for Fashion Designers

American Apparel & Footwear Association, wewear.org

American Sewing Guild, asg.org

Costume Designers Guild, costumedesignersguild.com

Costume Society of America, costumesocietyamerica.com

Council of Fashion Designers of America (CFDA), cfda.com

The Fashion Group International, Inc., fgi.org

Trend Union, trendtablet.com

Resources for Fashion Stylists

Association of Image Consultants International (AICI), aici.org

Association of Stylists & Image Professionals, asiplondon.com

International Fashion Stylists Association (IFSA), ifsaonline.com

Resources for Fashion Merchandising

American Apparel Producers Network, aapnetwork.net

California Apparel News, apparelnews.net

International Textile and Apparel Association, itaaonline.org

National Retail Federation, nrf.com

Resources for Fashion Media

Independent Fashion Bloggers, heartifb.com

Mediabistro, mediabistro.com

Teen Vogue, teenvogue.com

Women's Wear Daily, wwd.com

Resources for Models and Photographers

Fashion Photography Blog, fashionphotographyblog.com

International Models & Talent Agency, imta.com

North American Modeling Association, nama.ca

World Model Association, worldmodel.org

World Photography Organisation, worldphoto.org

Online Fashion Games

Fashion Fantasy Game, fashionfantasygame.com

Teen Vogue Me Girl app, megirl.com

Stardoll, stardoll.com

Style Me Girl app, play.google.com/store/apps/details?id=
  com.megirl.stylemegirl

12

glossary

agency. Company that represents photographers, models, or writers and helps them to negotiate work assignments and fees.

branding. Creating a unique image for your product, like using a specific logo or initials.

collection. Group of clothing created by a designer to tell a story.

colorway. The range of color combinations that a style or design is available in.

comp card. Card models carry with photos, physical measurements, and agency information.

computer-aided design (CAD). Software that allows users to create two- and three-dimensional objects and provide exact measurements for manufacturing.

contact sheet. A collection of photographs in thumbnail size printed on a single page.

draping. Process of placing fabric on a dress form and pinning it to create the structure of the garment.

dress form. A mannequin used by seamstresses and designers to drape and fit fabric for a design.

fashion blog. Blog that reports on the fashion industry and represents a personal point of view.

fashion house. Place where clothing is designed. Many times it includes many different designers who create a variety of product lines owned by one company.

freelancer. Person who sells work by the hour or by the completion of a project instead of working full-time for one company.

garment. Piece of clothing.

go-see. When a model interviews for a modeling job.

haute couture. High fashion clothing that is custom made and created by hand.

inspiration board. Often the starting point for a fashion collection or photo shoot. It often includes photos, colors, and artwork.

internship. Usually unpaid job in which you learn an occupation or learn from a particular person.

label. Product line or name.

lookbook. Collection of fashion photographs. These may be grouped by a theme like "back-to-school fashions."

masthead. List of staff, departments, and addresses for a magazine. Typically found on the inside front cover of the magazine.

nine-headed fashion figure. A figure drawing that is proportionally the height of nine heads from the top of the figure to the ankles.

on trend. Currently in fashion.

portfolio. Collection of work to show off a person's skills.

prototype. Full-scale model of a design.

ready-to-wear. Clothing made for retail stores and not for custom orders.

retouch. To improve a photograph by removing flaws.

sample. First sewn version of a garment or the clothing prototype used to sell the garment to retailers.

social media. Websites and applications that allow people to share information.

trimmings. Extra decorations added to a garment, like lace, ruffles, buttons, or beading.

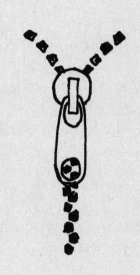

NOTES

*   BrainyQuote, accessed September 2013, www.brainyquote.com.

1.   "Fashion Industry Statistics," Statistic Brain, last modified July 27, 2013, accessed August 11, 2013, http://www.statisticbrain.com/fashion-industry -statistics; "Clothing Accessories Industry: Market Research Reports, Statistics and Analysis," ReportLinker, accessed August 11, 2013, http://www .reportlinker.com/ci02117/Clothing-Accessories.html; "Apparel Drives U.S. Retail Ecommerce Sales Growth," eMarketer, April 5, 2012, http://www .emarketer.com/newsroom/index.php/apparel -drives-retail-ecommerce-sales-growth/.

2.   Tyra Banks, "Thank You Tyra Banks!" Rafi Ridwan website, accessed March 26, 2014, http://rafiridwan.com/#!/thank-you-tyra-banks.

3.   Amanda Fortini, "How the Runway Took Off: A Brief History of the Fashion Show," *Slate*, February 8, 2006, http://www.slate.com/articles/arts/fashion/2006/02 /how_the_runway_took_off.html.

4.   Charlotte Core, "Haute Couture Fact File," Telgraph .co.uk, June 28, 2013, http://fashion.telegraph.co.uk/news -features/TMG10147014/Haute-Couture-fact-file.html.

5. Julie Ma, "Tavi Gevinson Is So Over Fashion (for Now)," *New York Magazine*, April 15, 2013, http://nymag.com/thecut/2013/04/tavi-gevinson-is-so-over-fashion-for-now.html.

6. *Teen Vogue, The Teen Vogue Handbook: An Insider's Guide to Careers in Fashion* (New York: Razorbill, 2009), 116.

7. Bethany Mota. Accessed March 1, 2014. http://www.cambio.com/2014/01/24/fashion-mogul-in-the-making-teenage-youtube-sensation-has-over/. Bethany Mota. Accessed March 1, 2014. http://www.aeropostale.com/shop/index.jsp? categoryId=28725626&cp=3534618.3534619.3534623.3541049

8. SearchQuotes, s.v. "Alexander McQueen," accessed August 29, 2013, http://www.searchquotes.com/quotation/I_think_the_idea_of_mixing_luxury_and_mass-market_fashion_is_very_modern_-_wearing_head-to-toe_desig/133614/.

9. Goodreads, s.v. "Rachel Zoe Quotation," accessed September 11, 2013, http://www.goodreads.com/quotes/635076-style-is-a-way-to-say-who-you-are-without.

10. Brad Goreski, "Sheer Terror with Coco Rocha," Bravo, April 11, 2013, http://www.bravotv.com/its-a-brad-brad-world/season-2/blogs/brad-goreski/sheer-terror-with-coco-rocha.

11. "Biography," Atelier Nicolas Caito, accessed January 7, 2014, http://nicolascaito.com/?page=bio.

12. "Success Stories: Nicolas Caito," *Vogue Italia*, August 4, 2010, http://www.vogue.it/en/talents/success-stories/2010/08/nicolas-caito.

13. Jay-Z, accessed September 10, 2013, http://fashionclub
.com/fashion/fashionquotes/page2.shtml.

14. Kenzie Bryant, "Gap Brands Take the 'Make Cute Shit'
Approach to Revamp," Racked, April 19, 2013, http://
racked.com/archives/2013/04/19/gap-brands-take-the
-make-cute-shit-approach-to-a-revamp.php.

15. Tom's Shoes. Accessed February 27, 2014.
http://www.toms.com/blakes-bio/l.

16. Alexis, "J.Crew's Jenna Lyons {Let's Quote!}," J.Crew
Aficionada, October 11, 2011, http://jcrewaficionada
.blogspot.com/2011/10/jcrews-jenna-lyons-lets
-quote.html.

17. "FIDM Library: Periodicals," Fashion Institute of
Design & Merchandising, accessed February 2, 2014,
http://fidm.edu/en/about/FIDM+Library/.

18. Mary Pols, "*The September Issue*: Humanizing the
Devil," *Time*, August 28, 2009, http://content.time
.com/time/magazine/article/0,9171,1919161,00.html.

19. Jenna Sauers, "How Fashion Blogger BryanBoy
Became a Front-Row Fixture," *New York Observer*,
February 8, 2012, http://observer.com/2012/02
/bryanboy-new-york-fashion-week-anna-wintour
-karl-lagerfeld-marc-jacobs/.

20. Moziah Bridges, "Who is Moziah Bridges?"
Mo's Bows Memphis, February 1, 2014,
http://www.mosbowsmemphis.com.

BIBLIOGRAPHY

Websites

All on the Line, imdb.com/title/tt1860385

America's Next Top Model, imdb.com/title/tt0363307

Andy Truong, andytruongworld.com

Barbizon Modeling, barbizonmodeling.com

Bill Cunningham, nytimes.com/video/on-the-street

Brad Goreski, mrbradgoreski.com

Bryanboy, bryanboy.com

Camp Fashion Design, campfashiondesign.com

Cecilia Cassini, ceciliacassini.com

Clothes-Line, ovguide.com/clothes-line-9202a8c04000641f8000
   00000af2821e

Clothes Show, imdb.com/title/tt0334839/?ref_=tt_ov_inf

College Foundation of North Carolina, Fashion Buyer: What They Do, https://www1.cfnc.org/Plan/For_A_Career /Career_Profile/Career_Profile.aspx?id=d8nRXAP2FPAXDx f2MSgzZKnlr0PXAP2FPAXgXAP3DPAXXAP3DPAX

Courtney Allegra, courtneyallegra.com

Crosby Noricks, prcouture.com/about-pr-couture/

The Empowerment Plan, empowermentplan.org

The Face, imdb.com/title/tt2390005

Fashion CAD, fashioncad.net

Fashion Club, fashionclub.com

Fashion Fantasy Game, fashionfantasygame.com/launch.php

Fashion File, imdb.com/title/tt0819856

Fashion Hunters, imdb.com/title/tt1879754

Fashion Institute of Design & Merchandising, fidm.edu

Fashionista, fashionista.com

Fashion Police, imdb.com/title/tt1676105

Fashion Star, imdb.com/title/tt1883661

Fashion Television, fashiontelevision.com

Flood Clothing, floodclothing.com

Glossi, glossi.com

Isabella Rose Taylor, isabellarosetaylor.com

Kell on Earth, imdb.com/title/tt1594402

La Miniatura by Jeffrey Sebelia, laminiaturakids.com
/about.php

Lauren Messiah, laurenmessiah.com

Lindsay Degan, degen-nyc.com/about

Lindsay Giambattista, lindsaygiambattista.com/About

Lives of Style, imdb.com/title/tt1809004

Makers, makers.com/tavi-gevinson

Nick Wooster, nickwooster.com

PopPhoto, popphoto.com/tags/software

Printfresh Studios, printfreshstudio.com

Project Accessory, imdb.com/title/tt1957484

Project Runway, imdb.com/title/tt0437741

PR Couture, prcouture.com

Rachel Zoe Project, imdb.com/title/tt1173677

Rafi Ridwan, rafiridwan.com/#!/

Refinery29, refinery29.com

Running in Heels, imdb.com/title/tt11385820

SCAD, admission.scad.edu/forms/requestforinfo
/LXFMeLearning?gclid=CPPSi6T-kbwCFQto7AodLGAAZA

Scott Schuman, thesartorialist.com

Seventeen magazine, seventeen.com

Sincerely, Jules, sincerelyjules.com

SiS magazine, sis-mag.com

Stardoll, stardoll.com/en/

Style, style.com

Style with Elsa Klensch, imdb.com/title/tt0126172

Susan Jeffers, susanjeffersphotography.com

Tavi Gevinson, thestylerookie.com

Teen, teen.com

Teen Vogue, teenvogue.com

Textile Exchange, teonline.com/
knowledge-centre/printing.html

What Not to Wear, imdb.com/title/tt0393009/

Whitney Pozgay, whit-ny.com

Articles

Banks, Tyra. "Tyra Banks Modeling Tips." *Seventeen*.
November 18, 2011. seventeen.com/fashion/blog
/tyra-banks-modeling-tips.

Castro, Tony. "Cecilia Cassini, Latina Teen Designer, Is Known
as the 'Mozart of Fashion.'" *Huffington Post*. August 8, 2013.
huffingtonpost.com /2013 /08/08/cecilia-cassini-teen-fashion
-designer_n_3725384.html.

Chi Lin, Joseph. "A Day in the Life of a Fashion Week
Model: The Hectic Schedule of Rookie Model Kel Markey
Reveals the Hard Work Behind the Breezy Runway Looks."
Time. Accessed July 7, 2013. content.time.com/time
/photogallery/0,29307,2019231,00.html.

Company. "Become a Fashion Stylist: What You Need to Know!"
Accessed October 2, 2013. company.co.uk/sex/careers
/how-to-become-a-fashion-stylist.

Cunningham, Erin. "Rad Hourani, The First Unise Couture
Designer." *The Daily Beast*. January 29, 2014. http://
www.thedailybeast.com/articles/2014/01/29/rad-hourani
-the-first-unisex-couture-designer.html

Donaldson, Aurelia. "Top 20 Fashion and Photography Books."
Telegraph. December 14, 2011. fashion.telegraph.co.uk
/galleries/TMG8950905/Top-20-fashion-and-photography
-books.html.

Effron, Lauren. "'A Model Life': Behind the Glitz of the
Modeling World." *abc News*. September 12, 2011.
abcnews.go.com/blogs/lifestyle/2011/09/a-model-life-behind
-the-glitz-of-the-modeling-world.

Fashion Fantasy Game. "Fashion Fantasy Game . . . Now a
Go-To Destination Site for Fashion Fans and Casual Gamers."
October 21, 2010. fashionfantasygame.com/press/10.21.10__
FFG_Runway.pdf

Fashion Fantasy Game. "Fashion Fantasy Game Reaches
Two Million Members." *Business Wire.* August 8, 2011.
businesswire.com/news/home/20110808006078/en/
Fashion-Fantasy-Game-Reaches-Million-Members
#.Ut_Uchb0AzU.

Fortini, Amanda. "How the Runway Took Off." *Slate.* February
8, 2006. slate.com/articles/arts/fashion/2006/02/how_the_
runway_took_off.html.

Freeman, Claudette. "Top 10 Careers in Fashion."
Catalogs.com. June 6, 2008. catalogs.com/info/bestof
/top-10-careers-in-fashion.

Hamdani, Sylviana. "Hearing Fashion's Call: Meet
Indonesia's Youngest Designer." *The Jakarta Globe.* December
8, 2011. http://www.thejakartaglobe.com/archive
/hearing-fashions-call-meet-indonesias-youngest-designer/

I SPY DIY. "How to Make an Envelope Laptop Case."
Brit+Co. Accessed November 22, 2013. brit.co/picks
/how-to-make-an-envelope-laptop-case.

Johnson, Beau. "Fashion School Rankings." Fashion Schools.
Accessed January 30, 2014. fashionschools.com/resources
/fashion-school-rankings.

Kee, Tameka. "Vivienne Tam Glams Up Stardoll." *MediaPost.*
July 11, 2008. mediapost.com/publications/article/86424
/vivienne-tam-glams-up-stardoll.html.

Kirk, Jessa. "Charles Frederick Worth (1825–1895) and the
House of Worth." Metropolitan Museum of Art. October
2004. metmuseum.org/toah/hd/wrth/hd_wrth.htm.

Knebl, Claire. "Designer Whitney Pozgay Talks Petite Styling
Tips and Her New Anthropologie Collab." *Teen Vogue*. June
2013. teenvogue.com/fashion/summer-trends/2013-06
/anthropologie-petites/?slide=1.

Larson, Kristin. "The Right Clothes for Your Body
Type: How to Find the Most Flattering Clothes for
Your Shape." *Real Simple*. Accessed August 2, 2013.
realsimple.com/beauty-fashion/clothing/shopping-guide
/right-clothes-your-body-type-00000000007925.

Lim, James. "Top Casting Director James Scully Calls for
the End of Anonymous 15-Year-Old Fashion Models."
BuzzFeed. June 24, 2013. buzzfeed.com/jameslim
/top-casting-director-james-scully-calls-for-model-covers-the.

Nastasi, Alison. "10 Essential Fashion Documentaries."
Flavorwire. September 7, 2013. flavorwire
.com/413746/10-essential-fashion-documentaries.

Northcott, Rauwanne. "Top Ten Cult Fashion Documentaries."
Dazed. Accessed September 21, 2013. dazeddigital.com
/fashion/article/16863/1/top-ten-cult-fashion-documentaries.

Pasori, Cedar. "The 50 Greatest Fashion Photographers Right
Now." *Complex*. August 2, 2012. complex.com/art-design
/2012/08/the-50-greatest-fashion-photographers-right-now.

Perri, Lisa. "Fashionotes 5: Top Teen Fashion Bloggers."
Fashionotes. August 5, 2012. fashionotes.com
/content/2012/08/fashionotes-5-top-teen-fashion-bloggers.

Peterson, Karyn M. "Making It Work: NY Library Hosts Own 'Project Runway' for Kids." School Library Journal. April 23, 2013. slj.com/2013/04/librarians/making-it-work-ny-library -hosts-own-project-runway-for-kids/#_.

Pierce, ShawnTe. "Teen and Pre-teen Fashion Designers Energize the Industry: The Industry Has a New Fashion Brat Pack." Yahoo! Voices. May 3, 2010. voices.yahoo.com /teen-pre-teen-fashion-designers-energize-industry -5940954.html?cat=46.

Pope, Marlena. "DIY Stenciling." May 14, 2013. *Rookie*. rookiemag.com/2013/05/diy-stenciling.

Popsugar Tech. "HP's Touchsmart tm2 Making Its (Project) Runway Debut." Popsugar. January 13, 2010. geeksugar.com/ Project-Runway-Designers-Using-HP-Touchsmart-tm2 -Season-Seven-7026999.

PR Newswire. "12-Year-Old Fashion Phenomenon Isabella Rose Taylor to Launch 'Adorbz' New Fall Collection of Trendy Tween Threads and Accessories." Yahoo! Finance. May 20, 2013. finance.yahoo.com/news/12-old-fashion-phenomenon -isabella-123500460.html.

Seventeen Magazine. "Lindsay Giambattista's Top 10 Amazing Life Moments!" *Seventeen*. Accessed August 12, 2013. seventeen.com/fun/articles/lindsay-giambattista-pretty -amazing#slide-1.

Singer, Maya. "Behind-the-Scenesters: Nicolas Caito." Style. February 7, 2011. style.com/stylefile/2011/02 /behind-the-scenesters-nicolas-caito

Tishgart, Sierra. "From Runway to Magazine: The Making of Teen Vogue's Fashion Week Trend Books." *Teen Vogue*. Accessed August 10, 2013. teenvogue.com/careers/fashion -careers/2013-02/fashion-week-trend-books/?slide=1.

Tucker, Kristine. "Careers in Fashion Journalism." *Houston Chronicle*. Accessed November 22, 2013. work.chron.com /careers-fashion-journalism-5422.html.

Wischhover, Cheryl. "Which Fashion Career Is Right for You?" *Fashionista*. August 17, 2010. fashionista.com/2010/08/which -fashion-career-is-right-for-you.

Books

Clerc, Lucille. *Flip Fashion: The Mix 'n' Match Lookbook*. London: Laurence King Publishers, 2013.

Coddington, Grace. *Grace: A Memoir*. New York: Random House, 2012.

Newman, Alex, and Zakee Shariff. *Fashion A to Z: An Illustrated Dictionary*. London: Laurence King Publishers, 2009.

Teen Vogue. The Teen Vogue Handbook: An Insider's Guide to Careers in Fashion. New York: Razorbill, 2009.

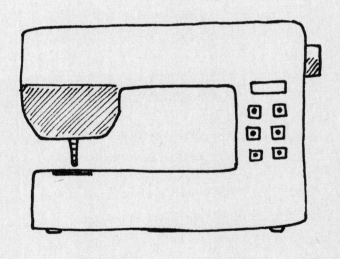